THE PROLOGUE TO THE CANTERBURY TALES BY GEOFFREY CHAUCER

MACMILLAN MASTER GUIDES

General Editor: James Gibson

Published:
JANE AUSTEN: **EMMA** Norman Page
ROBERT BOLT: **A MAN FOR ALL SEASONS** Leonard Smith
EMILY BRONTË: **WUTHERING HEIGHTS** Hilda D. Spear
GEOFFREY CHAUCER: **THE PROLOGUE TO THE CANTERBURY
                               TALES** Nigel Thomas and Richard Swan
CHARLES DICKENS: **GREAT EXPECTATIONS** Dennis Butts
GEORGE ELIOT: **SILAS MARNER** Graham Handley
GEORGE ORWELL: **ANIMAL FARM** Jean Armstrong
WILLIAM SHAKESPEARE: **MACBETH** David Elloway
                               A MIDSUMMER NIGHT'S DREAM
                               Kenneth Pickering
                               ROMEO AND JULIET Helen Morris

Forthcoming:
JANE AUSTEN: **MANSFIELD PARK** Richard Wirdnam
                    PRIDE AND PREJUDICE Raymond Wilson
CHARLES DICKENS: **HARD TIMES** Norman Page
GEORGE ELIOT: **MIDDLEMARCH** Graham Handley
T. S. ELIOT: **MURDER IN THE CATHEDRAL** Paul Lapworth
OLIVER GOLDSMITH: **SHE STOOPS TO CONQUER** Paul Ranger
THOMAS HARDY: **FAR FROM THE MADDING CROWD**
                        Colin Temblett-Wood
                        TESS OF THE D'URBERVILLES James Gibson
CHRISTOPHER MARLOWE: **DR FAUSTUS** David Male
THE METAPHYSICAL POETS Joan van Emden
WILLIAM SHAKESPEARE: **HAMLET** Jean Brooks
                               TWELFTH NIGHT Edward Leeson
                               THE WINTER'S TALE Diana Devlin
GEORGE BERNARD SHAW: **ST JOAN** Leonee Ormond
R. B. SHERIDAN: **THE RIVALS** Jeremy Rowe

Also published by Macmillan

MACMILLAN MASTER SERIES

Mastering English Literature R. Gill
Mastering English Language S. H. Burton
Mastering English Grammar S. H. Burton

MACMILLAN MASTER GUIDES

THE PROLOGUE TO THE

CANTERBURY TALES

NIGEL THOMAS
AND
RICHARD SWAN

MACMILLAN

First edition 1985

Published by
MACMILLAN EDUCATION LTD.
Houndmills, Basingstoke, Hampshire RG21 2XS
and London
Companies and representatives
throughout the world

Printed in Hong Kong

British Library Cataloguing in Publication Data

Thomas, Nigel
    The prologue to the Canterbury Tales.—
    (Macmillan master guides)
    1. Chaucer, Geoffrey. Canterbury tales. Prologue
    I. Title   II. Swan, Richard
    821'.1   PR1868.P8
    ISBN 0-333-37290-5
    ISBN 0-333-39298-1 export

CONTENTS

GENERAL EDITOR'S PREFACE

The aim of the Macmillan Master Guides is to help you to appreciate the book you are studying by providing information about it and by suggesting ways of reading and thinking about it which will lead to a fuller understanding. The section on the writer's life and background has been designed to illustrate those aspects of the writer's life which have influenced the work, and to place it in its personal and literary context. The summaries and critical commentary are of special importance in that each brief summary of the action is followed by an examination of the significant critical points. The space which might have been given to repetitive explanatory notes has been devoted to a detailed analysis of the kind of passage which might confront you in an examination. Literary criticism is concerned with both the broader aspects of the work being studied and with its detail. The ideas which meet us in reading a great work of literature, and their relevance to us today, are an essential part of our study, and our Guides look at the thought of their subject in some detail. But just as essential is the craft with which the writer has constructed his work of art, and this is considered under several technical headings – characterisation, language, style and stagecraft.

The authors of these Guides are all teachers and writers of wide experience, and they have chosen to write about books they admire and know well in the belief that they can communicate their admiration to you. But you yourself must read and know intimately the book you are studying. No one can do that for you. You should see this book as a lamp-post. Use it to shed light, not to lean against. If you know your text and know what it is saying about life, and how it says it, then you will enjoy it, and there is no better way of passing an examination in literature.

JAMES GIBSON

ACKNOWLEDGEMENT

Cover illustration; *Chaucer Reading At The Court of Edward III* by Ford Madox Brown, courtesy of the Tate Gallery.

INTRODUCTION

'The past is a foreign country: they do things differently there.'
L. P. Hartley

A person who travels to a foreign country may adopt one of several attitudes to the customs and traditions of the country he enters. He may seek to view it in relationship to his own culture, and tend to accept what he finds familiar while ignoring or avoiding what is alien to him. Or he may adopt a kind of 'colonial' philosophy, imposing his own system of values and beliefs over the native culture in front of him. Or he may attempt to understand and appreciate as much as he can of the country's own beliefs and attitudes, in order to understand how the inhabitants live and act.

At various times, all these approaches have been applied to Chaucer. We have had Chaucer the Comic Poet, valued for his humour, his bawdy stories and his benevolent social satire. We have had Chaucer the Humanist, who signals the movement from the Middle Ages to the Renaissance with his humanity, his understanding of people and their behaviour, and his realism. We have had Chaucer the Medievalist, a product of his time, seen as a serious, Christian and essentially conservative moralist. It is not the purpose of this book to state that any of these views (or any other) has some kind of unique validity, nor that any can be obviously discredited. Each approach has its own merits, yields different fruit, and indeed the reader with a flexible mind can gain something from all of them. However, as Chaucer is set apart from us not merely by the span of six hundred years, but also by historical, philosophical and aesthetic differences, we have felt it important to provide the reader with as full an understanding as possible of Chaucer in the context of his age. This book, as it were, is designed to act as a pair of spectacles through which we can see Chaucer, perhaps, as his contemporaries might have seen him. If the reader then wishes to take the spectacles off and view Chaucer in relation to twentieth-century concerns, that is of course an entirely satisfactory response. But to look at him solely through twentieth-century eyes may be to find a Chaucer who never existed.

One thing must be made absolutely clear at the outset, and it is something which should be - but rarely is - the first and last lesson of Chaucer studies. It is this: the study of Chaucer tends to lead to questions, not to answers; and the more one studies him, the more questions seem to arise. At first glance, the purpose of something Chaucer writes may seem obvious, and his attitude clear, but on closer examination the writing is seen to be more complex, the attitude more ambivalent. The purpose of this book is to act as a guide through some of the complexities and as a light to illuminate some of the ambivalences, but it will not ultimately offer many answers; the individual reader must decide about his own attitude and his own response. This lack of certainty and conclusiveness can make the study of Chaucer very challenging - and it should also make it very exciting. With many classics the range of response is often restricted by what is already beyond dispute; with Chaucer no dispute has been settled, and many individual responses can be justified.

We have tried to provide a way in which the reader can make the imaginative projection necessary to see Chaucer in the context of his age; once this has been done, it becomes easier to see his relevance to our times. The pilgrimage is a symbol of our journey through life, whether we believe in God or not, and the pilgrims represent the kinds of people we meet on the way. In Chaucer's characters we can recognise ourselves and those around us, and the way in which we respond to them helps us to define our attitudes to our own fellows. As William Blake put it in the eighteenth century: 'Every age is a Canterbury Pilgrimage; we all pass on, each sustaining one or other of these characters; nor can a child be born, who is not one of these characters of Chaucer.' It is in the continuing truth of this statement that the interest and greatness of Chaucer lies.

1 THE RELIGIOUS AND SCIENTIFIC BACKGROUND

1.1 COSMOLOGY

There are two fundamental concepts which underlie medieval man's view of his universe. The first is his belief that the Universe was created by God, and is therefore God-centred. The second is his belief that the Universe was coherently ordered, in the form of a hierarchy with God at the top.

It is this second belief that determines the medieval conception of all institutions. The Universe itself, the natural world, the State, the Church, society, even the human body were seen to be logically organised, with every element having its rightful place. This was an inevitable consequence of the belief that God had created everything, and that everything had a purpose. It was also immensely satisfying, because everything had its appointed place and its appropriate rights and duties.

This habit of mind was so deeply ingrained that it permeates all medieval thought and writing, and it can clearly be seen in Chaucer's work as well. In this section, we will see how the structure was applied in the case of the Universe and the natural world.

The Universe was understood to operate according to the Ptolemaic system, named after the Egyptian astronomer Ptolemy who devised it. In the centre was the Earth, and around it rotated nine huge transparent crystal spheres. The first seven of these each contained a single planet (the Moon, Mercury, Venus, the Sun, Mars, Jupiter and Saturn); the eighth contained the fixed stars; the ninth was called the 'Primum Mobile' or 'Prime Mover' which carried no planet of its own and was thus invisible, but which was thought to give motion to all the others. Outside the Primum Mobile was Heaven, unaffected by time, movement or change. The spheres were believed to produce a celestial music as they rotated – the famous 'Music of the Spheres' which is frequently mentioned in later literature, even after belief in the Ptolemaic system had disappeared.

This model of the Universe gives us some real insights into the medieval mind. Most obviously, there is the paradoxical humility and arrogance inherent in Christianity itself – the Earth is at the same time the lowest and smallest place, but it is also at the centre. The sun is of equal importance to the other planets (no Sun-worshipping here!); instead there is the sense that God's finger moves the wheel, the Primum Mobile. The Universe is at once awesome and impressive, but also finite and understandable. We need not be surprised that the Copernican system, which suggested that the Earth moved round the Sun (now generally accepted!), was so fiercely denied when it was first put forward in the sixteenth century by the astronomer Copernicus.

The same logic is extended to the natural world. All things in the Universe were organised into a hierarchical chain of being, the main elements of which were: God, the angels, man, animals, plants, inanimate objects. The last four constitute the four kinds of existence on Earth: mere existence (e.g. stones), existence and growth (plants), both these with feeling (animals), and all three with reason (man). Within each category there would be another hierarchy; for man it might be pope, king, nobility, freemen, serfs, or some more elaborate sub-division.

The splendid thing about this system is that it gave every object both a place and a purpose. The logic of hierarchy meant that the duty of every creature was to obey its natural superiors, and rule over its natural inferiors. Thus man must be obedient to the will of God, and must wisely rule over the animals and land he controls. Equally, a knight must obey his king, and rule his yeomen wisely.

If, however, a creature should fail in its duty, the whole fabric of the hierarchy would be upset. The angel Lucifer wished to be equal to God, and fell because of it and became Satan; Adam and Eve wished to be 'as gods, knowing good and evil', and in them the whole of mankind stands condemned for having upset the working of the hierarchy. Two centuries later in William Shakespeare's plays we still find that the murder of a ruler – Duncan, or Caesar – results in the disordering of Nature, with unnatural events taking place. Modern man, according to this view, might be guilty of failing in his second duty, that is to govern the natural world in a responsible and wise manner instead of exploiting it for his own advantage.

1.2 SCIENCE

It follows from the previous section that the purpose of science in the Middle Ages was fundamentally different from its modern one. Its medieval task was not to discover but to reveal. There were no 'new things' to discover, because everything had been ordained by God, but in all things God's plan could be revealed if one had the knowledge to do it.

For this reason 'scientific truth' was not of major consequence in the Middle Ages. What mattered was what had already been revealed, and this is why so much emphasis is placed on 'auctoritees' – writers and works of past ages that had revealed important 'truths' about God's will and His work. The fact that the Ptolemaic system is inaccurate was unimportant, as it was an effective model of the order in the universe. The fact that unicorns do not exist was unimportant, because they were an effective symbol of purity. It was known that the world was spherical, but medieval maps show a single disc containing land: it was the image of truth that mattered, not 'scientific' truth itself.

One consequence of immediate relevance for our study of Chaucer is that originality had little or no value for its own sake. Respect was accorded to something which had 'auctoritee' or tradition. Hence Chaucer very rarely invents his own stories, preferring established ones, and when he does apparently invent a tale (as with 'The Franklin's Tale') he actually claims to be merely translating it!

It is now easy to see why astrology was of such importance in the Middle Ages, and why alchemy and the study of medicine depended on it. The earth was subject to change; change was caused from outside; so unless events were the direct act of God, they must be related to the movements of the spheres and their associated planets. A study of Chaucer's Doctor of Physic will reveal how deeply rooted the science of astrology was, while the many astrological references scattered through Chaucer's work confirm this idea. It is perhaps food for thought that, while almost every other medieval belief has been dispensed with in modern times, the popularity of astrology is still evident in every newspaper, and even on television.

Although some aspects of the scientific outlook are dealt with later in the general commentary on the text, it is here convenient to summarise the most important information regarding the 'humours', the name given to the natural juices of the body.

All matter was thought to be composed of just four elements, each having two 'qualities' and a corresponding 'humour', as follows:

Element	Qualities	Humour
earth	cold and dry	melancholy
air	hot and moist	blood
fire	hot and dry	choler
water	cold and moist	phlegm

The human body was governed by its humours. If the humours became unhealthy or unbalanced, so did the body, and medical lore was designed to restore the proper mixture of humours in the body. In each individual it was likely that one humour would be predominant anyway, and this gave rise to the identification of various types of 'complexion' or 'temperament' – melancholic, sanguine, choleric and phlegmatic. Chaucer directly identifies the Franklin and the Reeve as being sanguine and choleric respectively, while the Wife of Bath is clearly sanguine too.

1.3 THOUGHT

As a consequence of the view of the Universe and Nature outlined in the previous sections, a habit of mind was formed which is once again fundamentally different from ours. This habit tended to expect and look for spiritual truths to be concealed in the most everyday items and events. Whole books were devoted to the 'spiritual' interpretation of the nature and behaviour of animals (books known as bestiaries), plants (herbals) and stones (lapidaries). Whereas the modern mind normally looks for a literal truth or a fairly simple symbolism, the medieval mind readily accepted complex and often concealed symbolism. In science this gave rise to the kind of books just mentioned; in art it accounts for the representationist or symbolic, rather than the naturalistic or realistic, nature of painting, with little interest in scientific perspective or naturalism when a wealth of symbolic significance could be contained in stylised and traditional forms.

At its most pronounced this habit of mind, when applied to literature, led to allegory, which is the extended interpretation of a narrative on a symbolic or spiritual level. Two of the greatest and clearest examples of allegory are the parables of Jesus, and John Bunyan's *The Pilgrim's Progress*. It was in the Middle Ages, however, that allegory became a dominant mode, and its most sophisticated development can be seen in the 'four-level' system of interpretation of the Bible, where each event was seen as containing not merely one but four kinds of truth. Much of the great literature of the Middle Ages is intentionally allegorical (for example, William Langland's *Piers Plowman*), but it was the habit of taking previously existing works and interpreting them allegorically which shows how important this way of thinking was. It enabled the Church to 'take on board' many of the great classical authors who were so much admired, for, although pagan, they could be seen to be unconsciously embodying Christian truths. The most famous example is Virgil's *Aeneid*, where Aeneas's descent to the Underworld was understood to represent allegorically Christ's death and resurrection. It is for this reason that the great medieval Italian writer Dante Alighieri, in *La Divina Commedia*, allows Virgil to act as a guide through both Hell and Purgatory, although, as a pagan, he is unable to enter Heaven itself.

Whether Chaucer's works can be understood allegorically is the subject of considerable and inconclusive debate. In a simple sense, it may seem clear that the basic device of the pilgrimage in *The Canterbury Tales* is symbolic of every man's journey through life towards God, in which case it is fitting that the Parson's sermon on penitence is at the end. To go a little further, *The General Prologue* itself may be seen as a progression from the Church Militant (the Knight) through the World (the Franklin, the Wife of Bath and so on) to Summoning and Judgement (the Summoner and Pardoner). Already here, though, there are reservations, and the situation becomes more and more debatable as one tries to push allegory further. But that is one of the pleasures of allegorical thinking, the discussion of what interpretations are and are not appropriate. That feature is evident right back in the parables of Jesus.

1.4 THE DIFFERENCE BETWEEN MEDIEVAL AND MODERN THOUGHT

Between the Middle Ages and the present day lie a number of events which have markedly altered the way people think. The Renaissance, the Reformation, the Industrial Revolution have all had their effects, but most of all it has been the growing ascendancy of scientific investigation over religious faith. This is not the place to trace the gradual shifts in modes of thought, but the results can be clearly seen.

Most essentially, we have lost the concept of a divinely ordained, hierarchically organised Universe. Gone is the arrogance which placed the Earth at the centre of the Universe, and we now have a more just conception of Man's place in the cosmos, but gone too is the sureness of order and position. No longer is our planet a servant for us to rule over; instead it is an environment with which we must co-operate if we are to survive.

The purpose of science is no longer merely revelatory, but investigative: it seeks to understand why things are as they are, and how things have come to be. It is this latter function which has changed thinking into an essentially linear process, a search for cause and effect. The allegorical habit of mind has largely disappeared, and we have adopted a mainly literal understanding of what we see. For example, in the Middle Ages the panther was taken as symbolically representing Christ because it was believed to have sweet breath; nowadays the panther is seen as itself, merely a creature.

Perhaps the most significant invention of modern science (although an accidental one) is the sense of linear time, of one thing coming after another. In the sense that the Renaissance brought scientific perspective into art, so science has brought us a sense of historical perspective, and ultimately that insidious machine, the wristwatch. We now place the whole history of the world in a linear order, and our own lives are measured out from hour to hour. In the Middle Ages, the situation was rather different: events might be thought of as 'long ago', but whether this was a hundred or a thousand years made no difference. Their own lives were measured cyclically according to the seasons, rather than in a linear manner. It was easier for them, therefore, to accept the Christian doctrine that, to God, all events are eternally present, and so Christ's crucifixion takes place every day as well as 'long ago'. To us it is more difficult to accept that a man who died in (more or less) 30 AD can also be being crucified at this present moment. It is no accident that so many symbols of medieval order contain the idea of circularity – the Ptolemaic system being a notable one.

We cannot, of course, adopt a medieval system of thought when reading Chaucer, nor is it desirable that we should. An author's work must be relevant to the reader's own experience, not merely an historical document. However, some imaginative projection or at least understanding is required if we are to succeed in our aim of seeing Chaucer as his contemporaries might have seen him.

2 THE SOCIAL AND HISTORICAL BACKGROUND

2.1 EUROPE

Despite the continual warrings, invasions and counter-invasions that occupied most European countries for much of the Middle Ages, there can be no doubt that, in certain vital respects, Europe was very much more of a unity than it is now, despite our proud claim to have a European Economic Community. The major factors governing this situation were the Church, trade, and even the wars themselves.

The Church
The influence of the Catholic Church over men's thinking has been examined in section 1 and its influence over their lives will be discussed a little later. Here we are concerned with the Church's two main contributions to the unity of Europe: a language and a culture.

For over a thousand years, Latin had been the 'common' tongue of Europe. Since almost all education was in the hands of the clergy, and the clergy spoke Latin as a matter of course, almost every educated man in Europe would have some knowledge of Latin, amd thus would have understood and been able to communicate with other learned men from every country, however different their native language might be. Much medieval literature was written in Latin, and would have thus been available across Europe without the need for translation. As late as Chaucer's own time his friend John Gower, who is thought of as one of the period's major English writers, wrote much of his work in Latin. As an agent for the transmission of culture and thought, as well as a unifying force which linked people of all European countries, the importance of the language cannot be overestimated. It is interesting to note how damning an indictment it is of Chaucer's Summoner that the most he can manage is a parrot-like repetition of 'Questio quid iuris'.

The wider impact of the Church on European culture hardly needs documenting, especially as its influence is still evident even in the twentieth century. The Bible and associated Scriptures form the whole basis of Western art, providing stories, artistic subjects and even words themselves for every artist in Christendom. While we now tend to lay emphasis on the secular writers of the Middle Ages, almost all literature, visual art and music was either specifically religious, or directly inspired by religious themes and material. Of Chaucer's contemporaries, Langland and the Gawain-poet are openly religious, while the moral concerns of Chaucer and Gower are everywhere apparent.

Trade

The rapid growth of world trade during the Middle Ages also acted as an agent for the movement of ideas and culture within the Christian world. While trade with Eastern countries led to an infusion of scientific and artistic knowledge from Arab and Asian sources, it was trade within Europe which formed channels through which all kinds of knowledge could flow. If one examines the contents of works like *Gesta Romanorum*, which were large collections of short stories, one finds stories from all corners of Europe, from classical and from Eastern sources all mingled together. Many of Chaucer's own tales are based on versions which derive from Celtic, French, Italian and even Indian originals.

War

War assisted the sense of European community in two ways. Firstly, since Roman times the national boundaries of countries had been constantly in dispute, and monarchs often had a most immediate interest in countries other than their own. England itself spent most of the Middle Ages fighting over possession of smaller or larger territories in France, and a single example will suffice to show the medieval attitude. King Richard I (1189-99), whom we like to think of as one of the most English of our monarchs, in fact only visited England twice during his reign, and is buried with his father, King Henry II (1154-89), at Fontevraud on the Loire in France – for these men were firstly Counts of Anjou, and England was merely one of their territories. In circumstances like these, we should not be surprised to find that, while nationalism might have been as strong as it is today, national boundaries were much more fluid, and cultural and social influences passed easily from one land to another. Chaucer was therefore as much a European as an Englishman.

The second warring activity which was openly designed to demonstrate European unity was that remarkable medieval phenomenon, the Crusades. Jerusalem, the spiritual centre of the Christian world, was won from the Moslems in 1099 and lost to them again in 1187; several successive Crusades failed to regain it. This is not the place even to begin discussing the complex reasons which underlay the Crusades, but one thing may be safely said: throughout the later Middle Ages they symbolised the unity of Christendom in the face of the pagan enemy, and on many occasions this meant the joining of Christian leaders and forces from different countries of the European community. It is against this background that Chaucer's Knight should be viewed, for the outstanding feature of his portrait is his crusading activities.

2.2 SOCIETY

This and the next section are closely linked: this section examines some basic aspects of medieval society, while the next shows how society was undergoing a period of significant change during Chaucer's lifetime.

Two features of medieval society are of particular importance in understanding Chaucer – the hierarchical nature of society, and its dependence on agriculture. As neither feature dominates modern life, it is vital for us to appreciate their significance in medieval times.

The concept that medieval society was totally dependent on agriculture is simple to understand. Its effects on people's minds, however, are difficult to grasp for a modern person who is 'protected' from the vagaries of Nature by advanced housing, artificial heating and the constant availability of food. Indeed, the introduction of frozen food has meant that the seasons have lost their significance in the availability of many types of food. Most importantly, the vast majority of people are no longer directly dependent on the land for their sustenance and income, and so have lost that simple relationship with Nature which was the automatic possession of the medieval person. To the latter, the effect of the weather was of prime importance, and the cycle of seasons determined both his activities and his prospects of survival. Winter for the medieval person was as hard a time as it is for birds and animals now, and his relief in spring at having survived was as great. The importance of the Invocation to *The General Prologue* hence takes on a stronger meaning. It should be no wonder to us that Nature was seen as a goddess during the Middle Ages, and one whose temper was always likely to be fickle.

The idea of hierarchy has already been discussed in section 1.1, but to see its relevance in society we need to look at the system known as feudalism. In essence, the situation was simple. The king theoretically owned all the land, and granted it to his nobility in return for service done to him (hence the Latin term '*feudum*', a knight's fee). The nobility had a similar relationship with others further down the scale, so that at the bottom the individual peasant might be a tenant on land held at several removes from the king himself. Although the system became enormously complicated as the Middle Ages progressed, and the original idea – land being held in return for service done – altered in a number of ways, yet the hierarchical nature of society remained. In a general sense, everyone 'knew their place'. It is noticeable, of course, that feudalism is based on land tenure; hence the agrarian nature of society is again stressed.

So far in this section we have been concerned with secular society and the way it was organised. We must not forget that there existed a parallel social structure – the Church. In the same way that the kingdom was broken down into shires and villages, so the archbishoprics of Canterbury and York were sub-divided into dioceses, archdeaconries and parishes. The individual's life was dominated not only by the natural cycle but also by the Church calendar, with its cycle of feasts and festivals.

Indeed, the Church formed almost a parallel and separate system of government to the king's own. The Church's leaders had considerable power over people's lives, levied taxes (tithes), and had their own courts, which operated entirely separately from secular jurisdiction. Chaucer's Summoner had the task of summoning people to appear before these Church courts. It is perhaps significant for us that the object of Chaucer's pilgrimage, St Thomas, had been a man who rejected secular power as Chancellor of England in favour of spiritual power as Archbishop of Canterbury, and had been murdered at Henry II's instigation because of this.

Throughout the Middle Ages the Church and State vied with one another for power, and at best lived in uneasy harmony. Chaucer's pilgrims, therefore, as well as being subject to the forces of Nature, also lived under two systems of government which between them shaped almost every aspect of their lives.

2.3 THE LATE FOURTEENTH CENTURY

During the fourteenth century, many changes took place which materially affected English society, and we will briefly deal with some here.

The bubonic plague reached England in 1348. In the great plagues of 1348-9 and 1361 a significant part of the population died, and this led to radical and far-reaching changes in every aspect of life. To imagine the situation one would have to think of a parallel where perhaps twenty million people died in present-day Britain. Before the plagues, as now, land was scarce and labour plentiful, so men were tied to their holdings and subject to their lords. After the plagues, land was plentiful and labour scarce, so that attitudes within society had to alter.

Again the parallel with modern Britain may be illuminating: if forty per cent of the population died, there would be no unemployment, no housing shortage, and the nation's wealth might well be more widely diffused. Conversely, many vital skills would suffer or be lost, and difficulties and shortages of diverse kinds would arise. The nation might emerge in fifty years' time looking slimmer and healthier, but it would be a somewhat different nation.

So it was in the fourteenth century. Social unrest after the major plagues led to the Peasants' Revolt in 1381, where rebels converged on London and the young King Richard II had to negotiate with them in order to retain control. Although the rebellion had little direct effect and was short-lived, it illustrates the considerable social tensions present in Chaucer's time, and the growing willingness of ordinary people to challenge the autocratic system.

This challenge was also developing in a more formal way with the growth of Parliament. By Chaucer's day the power of the Commons – mainly consisting of knights of the shires, like Chaucer's Franklin, and representatives of cities and boroughs – had grown to a point where they frequently challenged the authority of the king, who had to deal with them cautiously.

Further social change had been building up throughout the Middle Ages with the growing importance of commerce, and hence of the merchant classes. By the end of the thirteenth century there were already well over one hundred 'boroughs' with special privileges granted by the king, which separated them somewhat from the system governing the countryside around. In particular, trade associations known as 'guilds' came to have great influence over the life of the towns (witness the survival even now of 'guildhalls' in many towns), and merchants could become men of considerable wealth and power. It is only necessary to study Chaucer's Merchant and Guildsmen to see how this *nouveau riche* class was establishing itself during his lifetime. It is also amusing to note how accurately he pinpoints the pretentiousness of this group who, without noble birth, try to imitate the nobility in their way of life.

One other change in the late fourteenth century did not necessarily have a direct link with the plagues but was a process already at work in society. The Church, despite its degree of control, had always been liable to attack for abuses which marred its supposed purity. In Chaucer's time, three major figures stand out as voices expressing discontent – Wycliffe, Langland and Chaucer himself.

John Wycliffe, an Oxford philosopher, began a heretical movement known as Lollardy (or Lollardry) which challenged much of the conventional wisdom of the Church both in spiritual and organisational matters. By the time of his death in 1384, the movement had developed into an attack on almost every ecclesiastical institution, including monasticism, priesthood and the Mass. Chaucer himself is believed to have had Lollard sympathies, although the evidence for this is inconclusive. More enduringly, Wycliffe sponsored the translation of the Bible into English, making it available to the whole Christian community, rather than just the learned clergy.

Two leading writers of the time, Langland in *Piers Plowman* and Chaucer in *The Canterbury Tales*, launched attacks on abuses within the Church, and these attacks were both eloquent and, evidently, popular. As with the monarchy, the Church survived these assaults, but not unscathed, and eventually, of course, similar pressures led to the Reformation in the sixteenth century.

3 THE ARTISTIC BACKGROUND

3.1 REALISM

The medieval attitude to realism may be most clearly studied in the visual art of the period, and as illustrations are outside the scope of this book the student is recommended to find photographs of the works of art specifically mentioned below, wherever possible.

As has been suggested earlier in section 1.3, the medieval mind responded readily to symbolic values, and was less concerned with literal values than we are today. It was common during much of the Middle Ages, therefore, for art to represent religious doctrines through symbols, and it tended to be stylised and even at times abstract. The cruciform shape of so many medieval churches is a most striking example of this tendency on a grand scale. In visual art, we normally think of the lack of scientific perspective as the most characteristic feature of medieval painting, and this is entirely correct; there was little interest in realistic representation when it was the spiritual truth being conveyed that was felt to be important. For example, the twelfth- and thirteenth-century statues of the prophets in the porches of so many cathedrals (most memorably, Chartres in France) contain no attempt to make the figures look realistic or individual; instead their identity is proclaimed symbolically, with Moses holding the tablets of the Law, and so on.

As in so many areas (see section 2.3), it was the fourteenth century which saw a major change in the nature of art, and this change is of crucial importance as far as Chaucer is concerned. Whereas previously artists had tended to take spiritual truths and embody them in symbols, now they moved towards depicting worldly reality, through which the spiritual values could still be truly perceived. There was thus a gradual move towards realism. The progression can be clearly traced on tomb sculptures, which offer us abundant and dated evidence of how art changed. Prior to the fourteenth century the human face was almost always stylised, with little sense of individual identity; as the fourteenth century progresses, there is a growing individuality and naturalism. Even before the end of the century the artist Giotto di Bondone, in Italy, was working on the application of scientific perspective to painting. This introduction of perspective marks a shift in attitude from a concentration on the relationship between man and God to a concentration on the relationship between man and his world.

It is not surprising to discover that the continuation of this movement into the fifteenth century eventually led to a situation where the portrayal of the real world became an end in itself, and the spiritual impulse was submerged or lost. The movement culminated, of course, in the Renaissance, and if one compares, for example, Michelangelo Buonarotti's statue of David (1504) with the statues at Chartres mentioned above, one can see how far art has moved, for Michelangelo's work is a celebration of human, rather than divine, beauty.

For our present purposes it is significant to note that Chaucer was writing at exactly that moment when realism was asserting itself as a major artistic mode, even where it still served an essentially spiritual and symbolic intention. One of the major decisions which any student of Chaucer must come to is whether Chaucer represents the old tradition where realism serves a spiritual purpose, or whether he represents the approaching humanism in portraying real characters and real life for their own sake. It may be, of course, that he represents a fusion of the two, and that both impulses can be traced in his work.

3.2 ORIGINALITY

As has been previously stated in section 1.2, originality was not looked for in the Middle Ages in the same way that it is today, and in order to understand Chaucer we must know what was and what was not expected of him. For this purpose we can distinguish primarily between originality of invention, and originality of treatment.

Originality of invention was not normally an objective for medieval artists – rather the opposite. Respect was given to established tradition, to 'auctoritee'. The higher and older the tradition, the greater the respect, with the Bible being the auctoritee 'par excellence'. Thus a story clearly based on something from the Bible, or the classics, or a saint's life, had greater 'auctoritee' than one that did not. Most of Chaucer's tales are traditional in this sense.

Other factors worked against original invention too. There were no copyright laws and often little sense of authorship (see section 3.6), and texts were transmitted through copies made by scribes. These scribes often did not feel that there was any inviolability about the text they were copying, and might alter it to suit particular tastes and requirements. Thus art was seen as a fund upon which all could freely draw, and writers were expected to borrow or translate material already in existence. This is the very opposite of modern practice, where the least hint of 'borrowing' is likely to lead to virulent accusations of plagiarism. A fascinating example is offered by 'The Wife of Bath's Tale'. Two close contemporary analogues exist, one by Chaucer's friend, Gower, and one anonymous. A study of the three reveals that not only the story-line but even individual phrases are repeated from one to another, so it is impossible to judge who was borrowing from whom, or how far each writer knew the others' work.

Chaucer's tales have a wide variety of sources and analogues, and a study of them is a whole area in itself. For our present purpose, it should be said that *The General Prologue* has a particular interest in this respect, for it seems to be the most original part of the whole work. No direct parallel for the portrait gallery of individual characters has been found, and it is worth speculating how far the impulse for it comes from the new realism which was growing in the late fourteenth century (see section 3.1). It is not wholly novel, however; Langland's *Piers Plowman* covers the same kind of ground in a more general way in its opening section, and his description of the Seven Deadly Sins, although obviously more limited, has several close similarities.

If originality of invention was not greatly esteemed, originality of treatment was, and it was this that made an artist 'great' – whether he was a poet or an architect, supervising the magnificent new cathedrals of the Middle Ages. What was of interest was not so much the story, which was often familiar, but the way it was told. The Pardoner says in the prologue to his tale: 'lewed peple loven tales olde', and this delight was by no means confined to the ill-educated. A modern parallel might be the joke: however often we've heard a good joke we enjoy hearing it told anew, particularly if it is given some new twist or treatment.

The same is true with Chaucer. His gift, like Shakespeare's, was to take a story and mould it to his own ends, highlighting certain aspects and trimming irrelevant material. 'The Wife of Bath's Tale', mentioned above, is a fine example of this process which repays study.

Coming to *The General Prologue*, we find that its real originality lies in the treatment of the characters. They stand out fresh and vivid, and it is probable that some of them were indeed based on real people. In this way, *The General Prologue* is a highly characteristic product of the late fourteenth century, with the author revelling in the potential of new-found realism. It is here that we find a focus for the question posed at the end of section 3.1, which is how far Chaucer was motivated by a religious ideal, and how far he is the forerunner of the humanism of the Renaissance.

3.3 PURPOSE

What was the purpose of medieval art? In our own time, there is a separation between entertainment and instruction. Most entertainment makes little claim to be instructive, except perhaps in the crudest sense, and too much instruction lacks any entertaining aspect! In earlier centuries it was different, and the two were more inextricably linked. The Middle Ages took their cue from a verse from St Paul: 'For whatsoever things were written aforetime were written for our learning' (Romans, 15: 4). All art, however entertaining, could also be 'for our learning'.

There were many reasons why this should be so. Literature in particular was more closely tied in to people's lives, and had a social function, much as pop music has today; its performance was often communal (see section 3.7), it expressed group feelings and identity, and it dealt with matters and values which concerned the whole group. This was true for both the great epics like *Beowulf* and also simple lyrics expressing delight in Nature or love.

The fact that art was for most of the Middle Ages under Church control helped to stress its instructional side, for the ability to read, write and paint was often a skill taught by the Church. Much visual art had a practical purpose in conveying Christian doctrine to those who could not understand Latin or who could not read at all (most church decoration had this function), and there was a wealth of literature with direct moral or doctrinal content. More importantly, in accordance with St Paul's words, all art could be made functional, even if it was not originally so intended. As we have seen in earlier sections, moral or doctrinal meaning could be found almost anywhere: bestiaries revealed the 'meaning' of animals, the story collections known as *Gesta Romanorum* provided allegorical moralisations of well-known stories, and even classics like the *Aeneid* could be given a Christian relevance through allegorical interpretation. Above all, art necessarily represented life, and this meant God's creation. So in an inclusive sense all art could be seen as a celebration of something in God's world, and was thus purposeful as well as entertaining.

Doubtless there were exceptions, works composed without any sense of instructional purpose, but the normal situation can be seen in the Miracle Plays. These cycles of plays based on the Bible were 'popular' art in that they were performed by and witnessed by ordinary people. They involved everybody in the community, and were (and are) vastly entertaining; but at the same time they embodied profound Christian truths, often in subtle and intricate ways.

Similarly, the preponderance of moralising in much medieval literature testifies to the expectation that literature would have such a purpose, and there seems little reason to doubt that medieval people positively enjoyed such material. Saints' lives, in particular, were a perennial favourite, although they may seem dull and repetitive to us.

Again, Chaucer seems to be a characteristic member of his age. *The Canterbury Tales* contains everything from the coarse ribaldry of 'The Miller's Tale' to the formal sermon of the Parson. It moves from the courtly romance of 'The Knight's Tale' and the Christian legends recounted by the Prioress and the Second Nun to the crude realism of 'The Wife of Bath's Prologue'. It is all rightfully there because it represents that inclusiveness which is the fundamental key to the Middle Ages. There was no sense of impropriety in mixing the sacred with the profane, in the same way that both gargoyles and prophets adorn the walls of our cathedrals. It should be remembered that Chaucer's own *Tale of Melibee* is a sober moral work, and that although modern taste tends to dwell on the more entertaining and realistic tales and on *The General Prologue*, medieval taste was more catholic.

3.4 TYPES OF WRITING

There are two dominant features of medieval literature that are worth bearing in mind when reading Chaucer. The first is that the bulk of the literature is religious; the second is that most of it is in verse.

The first feature is immediately understandable, especially in the light of the comments in the previous section, where it was stated that the Church could bring even non-religious art into a Christian context by interpretation. It is noticeable, however, that even ostensibly secular material often tends to have a religious basis. Knightly romances could be non-religious, but we only have to look at a great poem like *Sir Gawain and the Green Knight* to see how such material could be used in the service of a strong and subtle Christian morality. More conspicuously, it is no accident that the heart of the Arthurian legends lies in the quest for the Holy Grail, a spiritual rather than wordly quest. The Grail was the cup used by Christ at the Last Supper, and it was believed that Joseph of Arimathea had brought it to England.

While prose was used a good deal for devotional writing, it was almost completely absent from fiction, and this can be understood when one remembers the oral background of medieval literature (see section 3.5). Poetry can be remembered and passed on; prose requires the ability to read and the availability of copies, so it inevitably failed to establish itself outside the Church until the development of printing and the growth of wider education.

It is for these reasons that Chaucer's tales are mainly in verse, and why so much of his time is given, explicitly or implicity, to Christian and moral writing.

Three modes of writing are also worth mentioning at this stage: Allegory, Dream and Quest. Allegory has already been mentioned several times as the dominant habit of thought in the Middle Ages. Two specialised forms which were used widely and effectively are known as the Dream Vision and the Quest.

The Dream Vision characteristically has a Dreamer as narrator, who can, under the licence of dream conventions, set forth narratives of all kinds which can usually be understood allegorically. Chaucer himself used the form in some of his work, but the greatest works in the genre are Langland's *Piers Plowman* and the poem *Pearl*, which is probably by the poet who wrote *Sir Gawain and the Green Knight.*

More important for us is the Quest, for here was a device which allowed for highly exciting stories, as well as a wealth of symbolic interpretation. Most of the greatest medieval works – *Piers Plowman*, *Sir Gawain and the Green Knight*, *La Divina Commedia*, *The Quest of the Holy Grail* – feature quests as a central device, and *The Canterbury Tales* is no exception. Although not openly stated as such, a pilgrimage is of course a spiritual quest, and Chaucer examines each of his pilgrims' progress. More will be said about this later in section 4.3.

3.5 LANGUAGE AND LITERATURE

No study of Chaucer's English is given here, as this should be available in any good edition. This section gives a brief outline of where Chaucer's language grew from.

Until the Norman Conquest in 1066, the prevalent language was Anglo-Saxon (or Old English), a Germanic language; Latin was available for the clergy and a few highly-educated laymen. Anglo-Saxon was a highly flexible and expressive language, and its literature was based on alliterative verse, not on rhyme or simple metre. Alliterative verse depends on the continuous use of alliteration within each line to give it structure and strength.

With the Norman Conquest came an abrupt change with the imposition of Norman French as the 'official' language, the language of the court and courtly literature. It was doubtless only ever spoken by a minority, but it affected everybody and meant that 'English' became a 'submerged' language for over two centuries. Popular literature must have continued unbroken during this time, but most of it was oral and little now survives.

By the fourteenth century, things were changing. During that century English re-emerged as the language of the court, of law and of literature, but it was now greatly modified by the admixture of French elements, and by Latin from its long contact with the Church. In the second half of the century came a great flourishing of English literature, encouraged by growing literacy and its recovered position as the prevalent language of the country once again. There was a spectacular if short-lived revival of the alliterative tradition by poets working in direct succession from the Anglo-Saxons, and this produced masterpieces like *Sir Gawain and the Green Knight* and *Piers Plowman*. A separate strand emerged with the appearance of writers like Chaucer, courtly poets whose style was a continental one based on metre and rhyme, and whose language was the 'new' English of London and the court.

This 'new' English was very different from that of the *Gawain*-poet, and its growing predominance during the fifteenth century meant that the alliterative tradition faded. This new English led on in unbroken succession to our modern English, and this is why Chaucer is the most accessible of all medieval poets for us, and why he is now most widely read. Indeed, for a long time he was the only major medieval poet studied, which is why he is sometimes called the father of English poetry. It is interesting to speculate that under different circumstances we might have studied the work of Langland or the *Gawain*-poet more readily.

For most of the Middle Ages, oral rather than written literature was the norm, for literacy was not widespread. In Anglo-Saxon times, poetry was composed by a 'scop', a poet who memorised, performed and handed on the verse of the period. The literature now remaining from this time has been saved by accident, written down at some stage for some reason. The same must have been largely true after the Norman Conquest. The line of popular literature must have continued unbroken, but we now know little about it.

As the Middle Ages progressed, a gradual change took place. The monasteries acted as centres of education and book-copying, and the extent of literacy and the availability of texts slowly grew. Poets became 'makers', craftsmen who produced poetry not only orally but also on paper. By the fourteenth century, the movement was so far advanced that we can really talk about writers and distinguish them – some are even known by name.

As so often, Chaucer stands at a point of change. He is now firstly a writer, and his work has all the features of a written literature. But many oral features remain, even traces of the alliterative style (see the commentary on The Invocation in section 5) and he himself, we know, read his work to the court (see section 3.7). It is worth examining Chaucer in this light and identifying oral features.

3.6 THE WRITERS

During the period when literature was largely oral, very little is known about the men who performed their work, and almost no names have come down to us. The fact that the poet was not so much a creator of new poems as a teller of old, a 'maker' (as the medieval term puts it), also contributed to this anonymity. What mattered was what was being said, not the person saying it.

It is not until written literature becomes normal that we begin to find the concept of authorship really growing, until by Chaucer's time we can distinguish many individual authors, and even discover something about their lives. Even then, much literature was probably still in the hands of itinerant professional 'makers', largely anonymous. The new literature was, inevitably, in the hands of the educated and the courtly.

Thus writers were often either clerics writing out of a spiritual impulse (Langland, for example), or sophisticated courtly writers composing for courtly audiences (most notably Chaucer and Gower). These people would not be professionals, and did not make a living from writing. Instead they might receive a kind of support or patronage from influential people, as Chaucer did from John of Gaunt.

On the whole, though, the characteristic situation of the medieval author was to be more or less anonymous. The perfect example is the poet who wrote *Sir Gawain and the Green Knight*. This poem survives in a unique manuscript along with three others probably by the same writer, saved as it were accidentally and largely unknown until the nineteenth century. About their author we know absolutely nothing.

In contrast to this anonymity, it is curious to reflect that with *The Canterbury Tales* not only is a good deal known about the author, but he even puts himself into his own work as a persona, and so we have not *no* Chaucer, but two! Nothing could be more indicative of the growing importance of authorship during the fourteenth century.

3.7 AUDIENCE AND PERFORMANCE

Clearly the audience for any work varied according to its nature and the situation; the Miracle Plays, for example, were witnessed by whole communities. We will consider here Chaucer's possible audiences and the different ways in which his work might be performed.

His audience was essentially courtly and sophisticated, for most of his poetry was composed while he was moving in noble and courtly circles, although even here the audience would consist of all manner of people from the nobility to the servants, just as Shakespeare's did two centuries later. We can separate the modes of performance into two, the public and the private.

In Chaucer's day literature was still usually a communal entertainment, and this tradition goes straight back to Anglo-Saxon times with the 'scop', or poet, reciting in the mead-hall. There is a fifteenth-century painting of Chaucer reading to the court of Richard II, and this was probably the primary means of delivery. It is at this point that Chaucer most nearly approaches being an oral poet, and his work takes on an almost dramatic aspect, with his naturalistic dialogue being most prominent and the complexity of his narrative method being most effective and subtle. It is interesting to speculate whether he was still sufficiently a performer to mean that he would adapt his tales as he spoke, according to audience reaction.

This public performance was, by the late fourteenth century, being supplemented by the growing possibility of private reading. With the increase in wealth and privacy for the leisured classes, it was now possible for favoured groups to enjoy their own entertainment. Little is known about this for sure, but small reading parties of ladies are mentioned in the Romances, where one person would read tales to a small group. This is similar to Giovanni Boccaccio's people in *The Decameron*, who tell stories to each other to pass the days in which they hide from the plague.

Additionally, there was even the possibility of individual private reading. Almost one hundred manuscript copies of *The Canterbury Tales* still survive, an enormous number for a secular text, and many of these must have been privately owned and read. In this way, the private communication from single writer to single reader (which we now take as standard) was being established during Chaucer's lifetime. It should be noted that Chaucer himself mentions both modes in the prologue to 'The Miller's Tale'. At one moment we find: 'What sholde I moore seyn', suggesting the oral poet speaking to his audience, and then just ten lines later we find him instructing those who do not want to read what the Miller has to say: 'Turne over the leef and chese another tale.' This is clearly a message for the individual reader.

So Chaucer's art had to be multi-purpose, and it is not surprising, therefore, that it is so varied. It had to appeal to all kinds of people from high nobility to the common folk of the court, and it had to be suited to both public and private performance.

4 CHAUCER

4.1 CHAUCER'S LIFE

Chaucer's life is much better documented than that of most medieval writers, and a brief account of it suggests why he was amongst the most innovative of fourteenth-century writers, and how he came to have first-hand experience of all classes of society.

He was born in the early 1340s, of a prosperous family of wine merchants whose rising fortunes and connection with the court gave Chaucer an excellent position in life among the merchant classes, which, amusingly, he satirises so finely in *The General Prologue*.

In 1360 he was captured while serving in the army in France, and the king himself contributed to Chaucer's ransom, an indication of his already established court connection. During the 1360s he saw further military service abroad, and during the next thirty years was sent on several diplomatic missions to France and Italy. This gave him ample opportunity to gain familiarity with all the latest developments in art in Europe, and to meet many leading writers. Also during this period he was appointed Controller of Customs in the Port of London, an influential position which must have entailed considerable experience of life in the City. Certainly he came into contact with most of the men of importance in London.

In 1385 he was appointed Justice of the Peace for Kent, and in 1386 he sat in Parliament as Knight of the Shire (like the Franklin). An appointment in Somerset some time later meant that he spent quite a lot of time in the country during the 1390s, but he retained his links with the court and seems to have enjoyed the royal favour of Richard II. He died in 1400, and was buried in Westminster Abbey.

From this outline of his life, it can be seen that Chaucer had direct experience of nearly all the social types described in *The General Prologue*, and that he was by turns a courtier and diplomat, a city businessman, and a countryman. There can be no doubt that this rich and wide experience was the main cause of the vividness and quality of the portraits in *The General Prologue*.

4.2 CHAUCER'S WORK

Chaucer's work is often thought of as belonging to three basic phases, known as the French, Italian and English periods.

During the first part of his career, he was most influenced by French literary traditions, which was natural considering the earlier domination of France over England, and his own experiences in France. During this period he even translated at least part of the great French romance *La Roman de la Rose*, which was a lasting influence on his own work, while *The Book of the Duchess* and some early drafts of other tales probably belong to this period.

In 1378 he made a second and extended trip to Italy, and his writing after this shows the clear influence of the writers Dante and Boccaccio. The latter's works, the *Teseida* and *Il Filostrato*, became the basis of Chaucer's own 'Knight's Tale' and *Troilus and Criseyde*, and the influence of Italian art on Chaucer's writing continued to the end of his life.

With *The Canterbury Tales*, however, which probably took shape during the 1380s, Chaucer entered a new phase where his own style was born out of the synthesis of all his influences. With this great work, which occupied him right through until his death, Chaucer seems to create a distinct English style, which itself influenced generations of writers after him,

As well as his longer poems, Chaucer is known to have written several lyrics, to have translated Boethius' *Consolation of Philosophy*, a medieval favourite, and even to have written a scientific manual, *A Treatise on the Astrolabe*. Even within *The Canturbury Tales* there is considerable variety, from the Parson's prose sermon to the Miller's bawdy comedy, and material from all phases of his development.

4.3 *THE CANTERBURY TALES*

The Canterbury Tales ostensibly concerns the pilgrimage made by a group of some thirty men and women, from London to the shrine of St Thomas, the twelfth-century martyr, at Canterbury. Chaucer describes each pilgrim in *The General Prologue* and at the end sets up a framework for the story-telling which follows. Each pilgrim promises to tell four stories, two on the way to Canterbury and two on the way back.

This makes *The Canterbury Tales* an example of one of the most popular of all medieval genres, the story collection. The idea of collecting stories into a unit appealed to medieval writers because it enabled them to gather often disparate material into a single body; it was, in other words, a good container. Story collections could be merely agglomerations of separate stories, like most modern collections of short stories, but it was more common to organise them according to some principle.

The most widespread example of the agglomerative technique was the *Gesta Romanorum* ('Deeds of the Romans'). This unstructured collection had each tale accompanied by a lengthy moral allegorisation to reveal its religious meaning, and was immensely popular in the fourteenth century. The sources of the stories were very varied – some were classical, as the title suggests, but many were added from Oriental as well as European sources.

Among the most famous structured story collections are the *Thousand and One Nights* (although this was not known, as such, in Europe in the Middle Ages), Boccaccio's *Decameron* and Gower's *Confessio Amantis*. The *Decameron* contains a wide variety of stories, as *The Canterbury Tales* does, but lacks an overall purpose behind its structure. The *Confessio Amantis* is a much more structured work, concerned with the education of a persona called Amans.

In many ways the story collection is an archetypal expression of the medieval love of inclusiveness, of 'putting everything in'. In the same way that a cathedral had a clearly defined purpose, and so could happily contain apparently irrelevant decorations like gargoyles and misericords, so the story collection could be marvellously varied without losing sight of its overall aim. Both contain 'God's plenty'. The scheme of *The Canterbury Tales* moves clearly towards the goal of repentance, expressed in the pilgrimage itself and in the progression of the tales towards *The Parson's Tale* at the end.

In fact the scheme, as can be seen from the attached table, comes nowhere near to completion, at least if one expects four tales from each pilgrim. However, almost all the major characters do tell one tale (four being unfinished), and although the tales are not organised in any final order one wonders whether Chaucer might have altered his original intention and decided to limit the stories to one per pilgrim. In this case, the scheme would be near to completion, although not finally revised.

There is good reason to doubt the effectiveness of adding further tales from each pilgrim. Often the impact of a tale is directly related to the character of its narrator; tale and teller are inextricably linked, as in the cases of the Pardoner and the Wife of Bath, for example. A second tale from such characters could not possibly have added anything to our understanding of them; instead, it would weaken and diffuse the effectiveness of the whole work.

The tales vary enormously in every respect, both in length, style and subject matter. The sequence begins with the Knight's tale, as is appropriate, and this is a long, courtly romance concerning the love of two brothers for a single woman. The pattern is then immediately and rudely interrupted by the drunken Miller, who insists on telling his 'low' tale, and this mirrors the unlikely assortment of pilgrims who are on the journey.

Although the sequence is not finally ordered, there are two definite fixed points. 'The Knight's Tale' stands at the beginning, which is fitting because of his social rank and moral stature, and 'The Parson's Tale' stands at the end. Most modern readers are surprised by this 'tale', as it turns out to be an immensely long prose sermon on Penitence and the Seven Deadly Sins, and its presence in *The Canterbury Tales* has been questioned, but it is surely the logical culmination of the whole work. The pilgrimage represents a quest of the spirit – it is fitting that the work should end with a sermon on the virtue of penitence from the most spiritually pure of all the pilgrims. It is also noticeable that there are many echoes of 'The Parson's Tale' throughout *The Canterbury Tales*.

#	Characters	Lines	No. of Lines	Tale	No. of Lines	Order in Robinson's Edition	
1.	KNIGHT	43–78	36	The Knight's Tale	2250	1	
2.	SQUIRE	79–100	22	The Squire's Tale	664	11	Unfinished
3.	YEOMAN	101–117	17				
4.	PRIORESS	118–162	45	The Prioress's Tale	203	16	
5.	SECOND NUN	163–164a	1½	The Second Nun's Tale	434	21	
6–8.	THREE PRIESTS	164b	½	The Nun's Priest's Tale	626	20	
				The Monk's Tale	776	19	Unfinished
9.	MONK	165–207	43	The Friar's Tale	364	7	
10.	FRIAR	208–269	62	The Merchant's Tale	1174	10	
11.	MERCHANT	270–284	15	The Clerk's Tale	1120	9	
12.	CLERK	285–308	24	The Man of Law's Tale	1028	5	
13.	SERGEANT-AT-LAW	309–330	22	The Franklin's Tale	896	12	
14.	FRANKLIN	331–360	30				
15.	HABERDASHER						
16.	CARPENTER			The			
17.	WEAVER	361–378	18	Five			
18.	DYER			Guildsmen			
19.	TAPICER						
20.	COOK	379–387	9	The Cook's Tale	58	4	Unfinished
21.	SHIPMAN	388–410	23	The Shipman's Tale	434	15	
22.	DOCTOR OF PHYSIC	411–444	34	The Physician's Tale	286	13	
23.	WIFE OF BATH	445–476	32	The Wife of Bath's Tale	408	6	
24.	PARSON	477–528	52	The Parson's Tale	Prose	24	
25.	PLOWMAN	529–541	13				
26.	MILLER	542–566	25	The Miller's Tale	668	2	
27.	MANCIPLE	567–586	20	The Manciple's Tale	258	23	
28.	REEVE	587–622	36	The Reeve's Tale	403	3	
29.	SUMMONER	623–668	46	The Summoner's Tale	586	8	
30.	PARDONER	669–714	46	The Pardoner's Tale	506	14	
31.	CHAUCER			Sir Thopas	207	17	Unfinished
				The Tale of Melibee	Prose	18	
32.	CANON						
33.	CANON'S YEOMAN			The Canon's Yeoman's Tale	762	22	
	TOTALS	31 + 2 + HOST			24		

5 THE COMMENTARY

The Text

Chaucer's poetry is meant to be spoken, rather than read silently. The words were, in the old sense of the word, broadcast to an appreciative audience at the courts of Edward III (1327–77) and Richard II (1377–99). We, today, need to re-create that sense of audience: we need to be involved in the active process of listening. To do this effectively we must hear the sound patterns, tune the ear to the rhymes and acquire some awareness of the assumptions shared by his original listeners.

Chaucer's English was full of sounds that we have lost. The word 'knight', for example, would have the 'k' pronounced, the 'i' sounded as in 'fish' and 'gh' pronounced as in 'loch'. We have to try to recreate the sound of medieval English so that we can hear the rich resonances of Chaucer's verse.

Two great linguistic and cultural strands that had coexisted in a stratified way in England since 1066 were merging together in Chaucer's lifetime. While Langland and the anonymous author of *Sir Gawain and the Green Knight* wrote predominantly in the alliterative Anglo-Saxon tradition, Chaucer rhymes in the French courtly style. His poetry is, however, scattered with alliterative effects, particularly when he is describing nature and the rougher aspects of life. We hear the alliteration in the 'w' and 's' sounds of the first line of the poem: 'Whan that Aprille with his shoures soote'. This fusion of alliteration and rhyme is an important part of the texture of sound patterns to be found in Chaucer.

One of the effects of rhyme is to produce a pattern of expectancy in a listener, which can be satisfied in several ways. If the expectation and the rhyme chime completely, there is a sense of appropriateness. If the poet deliberately disappoints expectation then the listener may possibly experience surprise or a sense of anti-climax. We will see later how much Chaucher relies on the patterns of expectancy created in the audience by his use of rhyme.

Another consequence of Chaucer's having an audience is that the poet could rely on shared assumptions and specific knowledge that a modern reader may have lost completely, or at best must painstakingly research. What was immediate to Chaucer's courtly audience is often remote and uncertain to us. Many of his pilgrims were probably based on identifiable individuals and recognisable types, so one can imagine the lively 'theatre' of audience response as Chaucer read. Some idea of this lively involvement can be seen in the way Chaucer's own pilgrims are made to react to the stories told to them along the way. Chaucer's words need an audience, and much will be missed if we do not listen to the words as well as merely reading them. There are several recordings available of Chaucer's work being read in Middle English, and it is worth listening to them to get the flavour of the verse.

The Invocation (lines 1–18)

Following the comments on the use of rhyme in the previous section, it is interesting to see how easily Chaucer's rhyme patterns accommodate the spoken sentence pattern that runs right through the eighteen lines. You will see and then hear a marvellous tension between the rhythms of a speaking voice and the stress requirements and sound patterns of rhymed verse. The effect throughout *The General Prologue* is of a naturalness, an ease of style which is at the same time shaped and given pattern and purpose by the rhymes.

Medieval man was much closer to nature than we are. We tend not to notice with such passionate enthusiasm and uplifting of the spirit the return of spring. For him, the coming of spring represented possible survival for another year. Spring was a triumph over 'the sword of winter'. In the text, nature is compassionate and restorative, the showers are sweet and the wind breathes benevolently. You might compare a more modern approach to spring in T. S. Eliot's opening to *The Waste Land* (1922), which deliberately draws in pointed echoes from Chaucer's Invocation. In *The Waste Land* April is the cruellest month, stirring memories that cannot now be achieved. There is for the poet a sense of lost potencies and a dissonance with the rhythms of nature. In Chaucer's case, the upsurge of the spirit is naturally and harmoniously linked to a religious purpose, to go on pilgrimages and give thanks.

The first part of the Invocation is dedicated to the natural mani-
festations of spring. April with its sustaining and sweet showers has
triumphed over the droughts of March, which are as much metaphorically
spiritual as physical. The whole landscape is emerging into life. The
soft breezes gently nuzzle life into the plants, and the young sun, with
all its promise of maturity to come, shines benevolently. The birds sing,
and, so urgent are their procreative instincts, they even sleep with their
eyes open.

Nature is on the move, and people too. Whereas birds respond to
spring in sexual terms, humans respond with an impulse of religious
observance, a wish to go on a pilgrimage. The primary emotion of the
Invocation is of an uplifting of the soul, a rebirth of the spirit as nature
pours its regenerative sap into the world and man sets off on a spiritual
journey.

This invocation is the most 'poetic' part of *The General Prologue*.
By the time of its writing, Chaucer had moved from the more formal
rhetorical devices that can be found in some of his early work to a style
that approached much more the patterns and vocabulary of speech.
Perhaps the most obvious device seen in the Invocation is personification.
This is more a medieval habit of mind than a literary device as there is a
natural tendency in medieval art to embody abstract principles, to
allegorise. Chaucer envisages 'Zephirus', the warm west wind, breathing
invigorating life into the young plants. The sun is described as young
and April is seen in a very strong physical relationship with 'the droghte
of March' through the word 'perced'. Notice Chaucer's extremely skilful
organisation of words here:

> Whan Zephirus eek with his sweete breeth
> Inspired hath in every holt and heeth
> The tendre croppes.

Through the word arrangement and the sound patterns there is an almost
physical equivalent of the wind gently seeking out the little nooks and
crannies of the copses and heath.

Another medieval habit of mind was astrology. For us the Ram is a
quaint, if not lost, reference. For Chaucer it was a significant sign of the
zodiac. Astrology was a serious science and the zodiac was part of an
enmeshing system that materially affected the lives of individuals and
the community. Particular signs of the zodiac had specific influences on
worldly affairs and exercised control over parts of the body and par-
ticular times of the day. The Ram was a symbol of sexual energy and

reinforces the atmosphere of regeneration to be found in the passage. Chaucer's audience would bring a whole complexity of responses to this line as well as a simple understanding that the sun is halfway through the space in the sky allotted to Aries, and the date therefore about April 17th.

One of the problems for a reader is to determine the exact tone of the line: 'Thanne longen folk to goon on pilgrimages'. Some commentators see it as a witty comment on the fashion for pilgrimages. James Winny, for example, says, 'The long opening sentence reaches its deliberately withheld climax – a satirical suggestion that religious pilgrimages are one of the rites of spring.' An opposing view is that the 'Whan. . .; Whan. . .;Whan. . .' construction heightens, in a way that is not at all satirical, the difference between the regenerative activities in the natural world and the religious impulses in the human. Those who had already travelled to the Holy Land and who wore a palm sprig in their hats to denote this, might seek distant shrines abroad, while Canterbury and the shrine of St Thomas was the particular goal for many pilgrims in England.

We soon discover that Chaucer's pilgrims do not all have the idealised piety of purpose that we might expect from the Invocation. However, they are setting out on a journey that on one level leads them to Canterbury, and on another level leads them, through a series of tales that illustrate the vanities, follies and possibilities of the world, to arrive eventually at the Parson's tale and Penitence.

Chaucer the Pilgrim (lines 19–42)

Chaucer now introduces his narrator. It is important to realise that the narrator is not Chaucer himself and we will see later on that the narrator has been endowed with the kind of neutral qualities that encourage the other pilgrims to reveal information and attitudes that they would hide from someone more robust in character. Chaucer uses the Host to supply the more coercive mode, while the narrator is given the sort of sympathetic ear that encourages the pilgrims to betray themselves through their confidences. For Chaucer's primary audience at court, there would of course be humour in the discrepancy between the known personality of the poet and the weakly complaisant quality of the narrative persona.

Artistically, the use of a persona is a brilliant stroke. It creates an illusion of reality which is reinforced by the fact that the narrator meets all the other pilgrims at the Tabard Inn at Southwark. It also enables Chaucer to make complex satirical judgements by having the narrator agree with, or report neutrally, reprehensible behaviour and attitudes in some of the pilgrims.

We learn that this gentle soul is ready to go on his pilgrimage 'with ful devout corage'. So, unless the comment is ironic, Chaucer clearly states his narrator's piety of spirit, whatever motive the other characters are given for going on a pilgrimage. The narrator's open personality is also stressed:

> So hadde I spoken with hem everichon
> That I was of hir felaweshipe anon.

The idea of a pilgrimage is important to *The Canterbury Tales*. At one level it may be nothing more than a convenient literary device, enabling Chaucer to use the assembled 'nine and twenty' as a coathanger for all the stories he had accumulated during his lifetime. At another level, he may have used the device to include a wide range of individuals and social groups as a more or less complete cross-section of society at that time. He may also have wanted the cross-section to represent the 'feld ful of folke', a token of all humanity, as in Langland's *Piers Plowman*, and the pilgrimage to reflect a progress through life towards the Holy City.

The pilgrims are assembled to go on a pilgrimage and to tell each other stories. It is important to see *The General Prologue* as the first part of a larger unit, and, just as each part of a cathedral, delightful in its own way, contributes to the significance of the whole structure, so Chaucer's *Prologue* is part of a literary unit and should be seen in the context of a journey to a Holy City and a series of stories that finishes with the Parson stressing the importance of Penitence. This religious aspect is often missed by those who study *The General Prologue* in isolation. It is like studying a triptych, a medieval painting in three panels, and, through concentration only on the scenes of this world in the central panel, ignoring the implications of Heaven and Hell which frame the central scene. So, while Chaucer's pilgrims assemble in a scene of realistic detail and atmosphere, there are rich poetic and spiritual reverberations in the idea of a pilgrimage.

The Knight (lines 43–78)

The Knight is one of those characters about whom you have to be careful. In essence, what you have to decide is whether Chaucer sees the Knight as a worthy man or as a mercenary killer, licensed by faith. Because Chaucer's tone is so often ironic, we have to be careful that we do not find reversals of meaning where none was intended. If we take Chaucer's description of the Knight as plain statement, we see him as an ideal character, a defender of Christian chivalric values, brave, modest and quietly spoken:

> And though that he were worthy, he was wys,
> And of his port as meeke as is a maide.
> He nevere yet no vileynie ne saide
> In al his lif unto no maner wight.
> He was a verray, parfit gentil knight.

'Worthy' is the key word in the Knight's characterisation. It is used to describe him no less than four times. Is it used to emphasise his worth, or is it like Mark Antony's 'honourable' in his famous speech in *Julius Caesar*, gradually accumulating ironic connotations?

If you choose an ironic interpretation, you will have to square it with Chaucer's seeming endorsement of those five knightly values: 'chivalrie, trouthe and honour, fredom and curteisie.' Chivalry, with its codes and obligations, lay deep in the medieval mind. The Order of the Garter had been founded by Edward III in the mid-fourteenth century and the Arthurian legends were almost the equivalent of our Westerns in the way they offered patterns for behaviour in a crisis.

You may be helped in your decision about the tone of this portrait by a consideration of medieval pespectives, which, whatever the historical reality, would in artistic terms be totally Christian. The Knight would be doing his Christian duty, defending the faith against the infidel. It may be that, scattered throughout the portrait, there are clues that Chaucer gives the Knight values and qualities that the author himself endorses. Right at the start, we might have a kind of touchstone character against which many of the subsequent pilgrims will be placed and found to be flawed. He is also at the start because he is the person of highest social status on the pilgrimage.

Through Chaucer's description of the Knight's service in 'his lordes werre' we are given some idea of the frontiers of Christendom – Lithuania, Russia, Asia Minor, North Africa and Spain. The fact that so many men had contact with different cultures must have eventually enriched European life. The fact that so many men spent much of their active life away from their homes explains in part the development of courtly love as a literary phenomenon.

Chaucer's Knight has spent a long time away from home. Chronologically, the earliest campaign was the siege of Granada (Gernade) in 1343, followed by the capture of Algezir in 1344. This campaign was led by Henry, Earl of Derby, who was the grandfather of the man who eventually became Henry IV (1399–1413), king for the last year of Chaucer's life. Between 1345 and 1360 England was at war with France, with campaigns not mentioned by Chaucer. However, in 1360 the Knight seems to have joined the Crusade of the charismatic King Peter of Cyprus who captured Satalye in Asia Minor in 1361 and Alexandria in 1365, and campaigned in Armenia (Lyeys) in 1367. The heathen lord of Palatye (probably Balat in Turkey) is documented as having a treaty of friendship with King Peter, who seems to have loaned him the Knight's service in 1365. After this, the Knight campaigned in Lithuania with the Teutonic Order, possibly returning in 1386 when the Lithuanians accepted Christianity. So when Chaucer says of him: 'And everemoore he hadde a sovereyn prys,' his supreme reputation was hard won and sustained over some forty years. Several of Chaucer's friends could have contributed to this idealised portrait of a knight. Three members of the Scrope family, Sir William, Sir Stephen and Sir Geoffrey all took part in the campaigns listed for the Knight. Two of Chaucer's Lollard friends, Sir Lewis Clifford and Sir John Clanvowe might have supplied the tone of moral integrity.

The details of the Knight's clothing tell us much about his character:

> His hors were goode, but he was nat gay.
> Of fustian he wered a gipon
> Al bismotered with his habergeon,
> For he was late ycome from his viage,
> And wente for to doon his pilgrimage.

He has good horses, but unlike many of the other pilgrims, he does not set any store by stylish and decorative clothes. His first act on returning from his latest campaign was to join the pilgrimage without finding the time to change out of his service clothes. Compared with the other pilgrims, he may be drab in his hard-wearing fustian tunic stained with the greasy and rusty effects of wearing chain-mail, but Chaucer shows these stains to be badges of honour.

So it may be thought that Chaucer is starting the descriptions of the pilgrims with a model, a standard against which others will be judged. Where the Knight is prudent, others are reckless; where he is humble, others are aggressively arrogant and self-opinionated. Here is a man who has subjugated his individuality to service and put his duty, both as a warrior and as a pilgrim, before reward and external appearance.

If you are looking for two simple ways of gauging Chaucer's attitude towards his characters you may find it useful to consider the ideas of service and self. Characters like the Knight, the Clerk, the Parson and the Plowman are not treated ironically. These have all dedicated their lives to the service of their God, their country, their quest for learning, their parish and their neighbour. In this dedication, they have submerged their identities. Notice how so many of the other pilgrims are concerned about manners, clothes and their own self-importance, or, worst of all, have diverted their opportunities for exercising their duty into chances for self-indulgence and profit.

The Squire (lines 79–100)

It was ordained in the manuals on knighthood that a knight should travel accompanied, at the minimum, by his squire and another servant. In this case, the Squire is the Knight's son, and the sober achievements of the father are balanced against the light-hearted potential of the Squire. While the Knight is involved in 'his lordes werre', the Squire fights 'in hope to stonden in his lady grace'. This is a portrait impregnated with courtly values and the traditions of courtly love. With his 'lokkes crulle' the Squire typifies the hero in courtly romances, and in his skills of riding, jousting, dancing, drawing and writing, together with his humility and sense of duty towards his father, he shows the ideal qualities of a young squire. The narrator is gently and good-humouredly understanding of the Squire's passion for love:

> So hoote he lovede that by nightertale
> He sleep namoore than dooth a nightingale.

Just like the birds in the Invocation!

In all, he behaves as he should behave, within the prescription for his rank. There is, perhaps, just a hint of nostalgia showing through the portrait. Chaucer himself served as a squire: 'In Flaundres, in Artois, and Picardie,' where he was captured in 1360 by the French and then ransomed by Edward III.

Just as 'worthy' is the key adjective to describe the Knight, so 'fressh' is the word most often used to describe the Squire. With its associations of clean, smart and lively, you can understand why it is one of the standard adjectives for heroes in courtly romances. In a society where marriage was arranged, where husbands were often smelly, absent or interested only in producing a son and heir from the marriage, it is not surprising that a literature developed in which women were placed on pedestals, worshipped from afar by men whose sole wish was to serve and accept whatever grace the lady might dispense.

The medieval mind was fascinated by decoration. Look at any page of manuscript and you will find decorative emblems often taking up more space than the words. Compare the Squire:

> Embrouded was he, as it were a meede
> Al ful of fresshe floures, white and reede.

He is delightfully embroidered, the flowers significant in their colours: white for purity, red for passion. All the exuberant and joyous energy of the 'lusty bachelor' serving out his probation for knighthood is summed up in that splendidly evocative line: 'He was as fressh as is the month of May'. Chaucer has described in this portrait a natural, vital energy, but an energy that is directed and aware of social and filial obligation:

> Curteis he was, lowely, and servisable,
> And carf biforn his fader at the table.

The Yeoman (lines 101–17)

Like everything else associated with the Knight, the Yeoman expresses his function. He is a silent craftsman, well-turned out and competent: 'Wel koude he dresse his takel yemanly'. He seems to be a servant and a forester. Perhaps in times of war and travel he looked after the Knight, and during rare and isolated moments of peace he protected the deer in the royal forests. Certainly his medallion of St Christopher protected him in each circumstance, as both travellers and foresters claimed him as their patron saint. The Yeoman is not allotted any story, and he is not mentioned again in any of the links between stories, but Chaucer's art creates a memorable character. He stands out clearly and through his silences we catch his taciturn strength.

The characterisation is built up by using significant details. Green was the colour traditionally associated with foresters and verderers (game-wardens), and Chaucer stresses the trim and economical efficiency of a person who has pared from his personality everything that detracts from his function. The arrows are sharp and well-flighted. There is some controversy as to the relative merits of goose and peacock feathered flights, but there seems little doubt that Chaucer saw the peacock feathers, and the way they were trimly set out from the shaft, as marks of efficiency. The rest of his equipment, his 'mighty bowe', his decorated wristguard, his sword, shield and finely mounted dagger are all expressive of his function and quality. He carries a horn which was used to call the various stages of the hunt, suspended from a diagonal shoulder-strap. Perhaps the best line to show Chaucer's ability to convey, with an efficiency the Yeoman himself would respect, a very clear visual impression of the man's appearance is: 'A not heed hadde he, with a broun visage'. The appropriateness of a nut as a metaphor for the hard and tanned quality of his shaven head, the woodland associations of the word itself, are all obvious and immediate. What might be less obvious is the contribution of the sound patterns to the sense. It is not too fanciful to hear the para-rhymes (similar consonants, different vowel sounds) in 'heed' and 'hadde' and the completion of the unit with the final 'he' suggests toughness both of body and perhaps character. The last part of the line, with its associations of health and the great outdoors, reinforces the effects of the natural world on a man whose integrity is delineated in every word used to describe him. He is in all ways an appropriate servant to the Knight and his Squire.

The Prioress (lines 118–62)

The Prioress is the first of another group of three, a kind of anti-trio to the Knight's group. Here we have three religious deviants who might in various ways represent the sins of the World, the Flesh and the Devil, which were according to medieval thinking the three traditional enemies of mankind. In the portraits of the Squire and Yeoman, we notice how descriptive points of detail become hangers for endorsement or gentle fun. With this next group the details are, to varying degrees, used to show how far the characters have deviated from how they should behave. The fascinating thing is to see how Chaucer establishes the norm and how he uses both the narrator and his own attitude to create patterns of judgement.

Much of the first part of the description of the Prioress is gentle comment. She is given the somewhat dubious name of 'madame Eglantine' with its associations with heroines in courtly romances. This, together with the fact that she, as a Prioress, should not be on a pilgrimage, begins to suggest some duality in the characterisation. With her elegant oaths and her self-conscious concern to do everything well by reference to external standards, she is a great 'seemer': 'In curteisie was set ful muchel hir lest,' and she took pains to 'countrefete cheere of court'.

So far, though, it is only her style of speaking and eating that is teased. This slightly worldly creature is perhaps a bit pathetic in her concerns but Chaucer's tone hardens as we consider the implications of her 'conscience'. This was not directed towards people, but towards animals and her dogs. With almost criminal largess she fed her dogs on wastel bread, which only the rich could afford. With the social conditions prevailing that gave rise to The Peasants' Revolt of 1381, this would not be a lost point for some of Chaucer's audience. However, equally significant would be the fact that Chaucer, and many of his audience, would have read or been aware of a manual on how to bring up daughters written by the Chevalier de la Tour Landry. One of the moral stories in the book is of a lady-in-waiting who fed her dogs well but who allowed the poor to famish. After her death, she is licked by her dogs until her body becomes as black as coal. So much for the Prioress's elegant concerns then!

In all this, the tone of the narrator has not changed. But the details selected, and the background against which they are set, modify quite considerably our attitude towards the character. The straightforward endorsement from the complaisant narrator becomes a strong irony from Chaucer the poet. Thus while the narrator is defending the 'harmless' nature of her oath because it is merely by 'Seinte Loy', Chaucer knows that his audience was aware that prioresses should not swear at all. Similarly, the French that the narrator praises her for speaking 'ful faire and fetisly' would be recognised by a courtly audience as being inferior to the French of Court. Furthermore, while the narrator singles out for praise her charitable and pitying nature, the audience is made aware of its total misdirection towards animals. The technique for achieving this is one that we often find in Chaucer – a seemingly straightforward commendation such as: 'And Frenssh she spak ful faire and fetisly,' is immediately undercut by a line which alters the impression: 'After the scole of Stratford atte Bowe'. The narrator may not notice the import of what he says, but the audience does.

A similar subtlety can be noticed in the description of her physical attributes:

> Ful semely hir wimpul pinched was,
> Hir nose tretis, hir eyen greye as glas,
> Hir mouth ful smal, and therto softe and reed;
> But sikerly she hadde a fair forheed;
> It was almoost a spanne brood, I trowe;

For, hardily, she was nat undergrowe.
Ful fetis was hir cloke, as I was war.
Of smal coral aboute hire arm she bar
A peire of bedes, gauded al with grene,
And theron heng a brooch of gold ful sheene,
On which ther was first write a crowned A,
And after 'Amor vincit omnia'.

This extract confirms all our suspicions about her sense of priorities. She has modified her wimple so that it is elegantly pleated to frame all the attributes of medieval beauty which the Prioress is so lucky to possess and so determined to show off to maximum advantage to the admiring world. The finely shaped nose, the grey-blue eyes, the broad forehead and her figure are all enhanced by the cut of her clothes. The narrator is evidently attracted to her – note the way that he lingers on the provocative glamour of 'Hir mouth ful smal, and therto softe and reed', and is aware of the woman beneath the cloak: 'For hardily, she was nat undergrowe'.

A modern reader too might well enjoy the fact that the Prioress's femininity cannot be repressed by her function, but there seems little doubt that Chaucer wants us to evaluate her more critically. A medieval audience might well interpret details such as her broad forehead, her shapely nose and her soft mouth as signs of a worldly rather than spiritual nature, and Chaucer finishes the description by drawing our attention to the symbolically decorated rosary and the pointed ambiguity of the motif on her brooch. Just what kind of love is it in her case that does conquer all? This last line illustrates the delicate balance that Chaucer achieves between subtle irony and human understanding of the predicament of a worldly woman caught in a spiritual vocation. The Prioress is misplaced, but she is not evil; you should compare the tone of this portrait with that of the following ones, where the satirical emotion is less tempered by compassion.

The Monk (lines 165–207)

The portrait and comment on the Monk is of a more robust orchestration. All his delights are of a royal nature. He loves hunting, fine fur-trimmed clothes and roast swan. As the Prioress surrendered her obligations to the standards and valuations of the World, so the Monk is, in his hunting and eating, a seeker of the Flesh, at the expense of those duties which should keep him in his cloisters:

> Of priking and of hunting for the hare
> Was al his lust, for no cost wolde he spare.

Not for this man the old rules of Saint Maurus or of Saint Benedict. He found these too constricting and 'heeld after the newe world the space'. He totally rejected any biblical condemnation of hunting and any ruling that confined him to studying and labouring 'as Austin bit'. With a forthright defiance of rules and regulations, 'Therfore he was a prikasour aright'.

His clothes and appearance are those of the self-indulgent man. He carries further the kind of embellishing previously noted in the description of the Prioress:

> I seigh his sleves purfiled at the hond
> With gris, and that the fineste of a lond.

The same ambiguity about human and divine love seen in the Prioress's brooch is also evident in the love-knot sported by the Monk to fasten his hood. Most importantly, his physical description shows us a man who puts his own well-being first: 'He was a lord ful fat and in good point'. In fact, for this man the sound of his bridle would have more significance than the sound of the chapel bell. Perhaps Chaucer is catching the tensions between the Church as a political institution and the Church as a divine instrument of God's salvation – the Monk is an 'outridere' whose attention is turned towards administrative rather than spiritual concerns:

> He yaf nat of that text a pulled hen,
> That seith that hunters ben nat hooly men,
> Ne that a monk, whan he is recchelees,
> Is likned til a fissh that is waterlees,–
> This is to seyn, a monk out of his cloistre.
> But thilke text heeld he nat worth an oystre;
> And I seyde his opinion was good.

There is little doubt of Chaucer's attitude here. He makes the narrator agree with the Monk's dismissal of the authorised and appropriate patterns of behaviour for his calling, but the effect is of a firm indictment of the Monk and his ways. You first notice in this extract the lively and colloquial language. There is an aggressively dismissive note to 'a pulled hen' and 'nat worth an oystre'. They seem indirect quotations of the Monk and certainly do not fit the meekly compliant tone

Chaucer gives his narrator at this point. The Monk shows scant regard for authority and shows no qualms about setting himself above the accumulated and ordained wisdom of his order. The questions:

> What sholde he studie and make himselven wood,
> Upon a book in cloistre alwey to poure,
> Or swinken with his handes, and laboure,
> As Austin bit? How shal the world be served?

are all rhetorical and their implied answers indict the Monk. The Monk has condemned himself through his own reported opinions.

It might be useful at this point to consider in a little bit more detail the role of Chaucer's narrator in the *Prologue*. We perhaps might understand better if we examine how the narrator in another great work by Chaucer, *Troilus and Criseyde*, changes his opinions towards his material as he proceeds with the telling. The process of narration has taught him wisdom. At the beginning of *Troilus and Criseyde*, the storyteller is much involved with the success or failure of the love between Troilus and Criseyde. By the end, having learned from the story, he urges his audience to:

> Repeyreth hom fro wordly vanyte,
> And of youre herte up casteth the visage
> To thilke God that after his ymage
> Yow made, and thynketh al nys but a faire
> This world, that passeth soone as floures faire.

You could not argue that the narrator of the *Prologue* acquires such wisdom, but it may be helpful to see the narrator as a useful persona to whom Chaucer gives the same faulty judgement as the rest of us. In any event we must see the narrator as separate from Chaucer and look for other places where the poet produces complex effects from that separateness.

The Friar (lines 208–69)

The last of this particular group of religious deviants, who set their own wishes against ordained patterns of behaviour, is by far the worst. Friars were already notorious for their excesses, for they had moved a long way from the piety of purpose enshrined in their original practices. They were supposed to be itinerant teachers and defenders of the

Catholic faith, combating heresy; in many cases they had become exploiters of the poor and parasites on both community and Church. Every detail in this portrait offered by the bland narrator is an indictment and the whole passage generates a savage but controlled indignation, equalled perhaps only by the great satirical writers, Alexander Pope and Jonathan Swift.

We should be warned at the start by the three adjectives 'wantowne', 'merie' and 'solempne'. They are just jumbled together by the narrator and, in a way, that kind of moral chaos is appropriate to the character of the Friar. What seems a fine gesture in making marriages at 'his owene cost' becomes a despicable motive to offload his own sexual mistakes. The line: 'Unto his ordre he was a noble post' becomes grimly inverted by irony. It is difficult to imagine anything less like a pillar of the community than this man. Adverbs like 'swetely' and adjectives like 'plesaunt' hang corrosively. Chaucer is often an ironic writer: rarely is he so intensely ironic as in this portrait.

> Therfore in stede of wepinge and preyeres
> Men moote yeve silver to the povre freres.

This man abuses his power of confession:

> He was an esy man to yeve penaunce,
> Ther as he wiste to have a good pitaunce,

in contrast to the Parson who would 'snibben sharply for the nonis' anyone who transgressed, regardless of social position. We get a clear idea of the Friar's social priorities in the following lines:

> He knew the tavernes wel in every toun
> And everich hostiler and tappestere
> Bet than a lazar or a beggestere.

This irascible, two-faced exploiter of poor widows, while he could be angry and rage 'as it were right a whelp', could produce in a variety of situations a dangerous illusion of sweetness and integrity:

> Somwhat he lipsed, for his wantownesse,
> To make his Englissh sweete upon his tonge,

and

> For thogh a widwe hadde noght a sho,
> So plesaunt was his 'In principio',
> Yet wolde he have a ferthing, er he wente.

Part of Chaucer's criticism of the previous two characters is that they have shifted from ordained practice. With the Friar, the criticism seems to be on a different level. There is a fundamental evil at the core of the Friar, an evil made worse because it seems so plausible and he so 'worthy'. These are the qualities of the Devil himself.

Perhaps the most damning indictment of the Friar and his practices comes in these lines:

> It is nat honest, it may nat avaunce,
> For to deelen with no swich poraille,
> But al with riche and selleres of vitaille.
> And over al, ther as profit sholde arise,
> Curteis he was and lowely of servise.
> Ther nas no man nowher so vertuous.

This extract conveys well the lashing intensity of Chaucer's irony. The narrator (neutrally) reports the language and, through that, the attitude of the Friar. 'Honest' with its range of meanings is powerfully ambiguous because it links 'honourable' with 'respectable'. However, there is no uncertainty as to tone and meaning with 'swich poraille'. The Friar thinks the needy poor are rabble and scum. That arrogance disappears the moment there is a chance to make money:

> Ful wel biloved and famulier was he
> With frankeleyns over al in his contree,
> And eek with worthy wommen of the toun.

Then, he assumes an ingratiating humility and the narrator comments in an emphatic triple negative:

> Ther nas nowher no man so vertuous.

The naïve manner of the narrator stands in sharp contrast to the indignation shown by Chaucer, and should, when set against the brazen details of the Friar's depravity, ignite the disgust of the audience. In its context it is one of Chaucer's most devastating single lines.

The Merchant (lines 270–84)

After the description of the Friar, there is a definite change in the tone and scope of presentation and appraisal. We meet a group of pilgrims who seem to have mastered the art of social deception and who seem very different from what they in fact are. Embedded in their midst is the Clerk, who by contrast acts as a yardstick against whom others are tested and found wanting.

The Merchant is the first of several whose façade of self-importance is exposed to scrutiny. For this man the world seems to begin and end with himself and his own shadow:

> His resons he spak ful solempnely,
> Sowninge alwey th'encrees of his winning.

Every detail about him, from his high saddle, his imported beaver hat and his expensive boots is chosen to enhance his status. He is described as a 'worthy' man, but the word has been drastically and ironically re-valued since it was first used to describe the Knight. One can imagine this creature, pompous, boring, sounding 'terribly' significant to himself with his skilful and devious financial dealings, creating an illusion of affluence so that: 'Ther wiste no wight that he was in dette'.

Chaucer's audience would be quick to spot that each of his major financial transactions was highly irregular. It was illegal to 'in eschaunge sheeldes selle' (dealing in foreign currency), and 'bargaines' and 'chevis-saunce' refer to devices which enabled financiers to overcome the strict laws against money-lending for profit. The Merchant's one abiding external concern is that the crossing between Middleburg and Orwell should be kept open so that his particular trade (exporting cloth) could flourish.

This monument to self-worship, 'so estatly. . .of his governaunce', is devastatingly deflated by the fact that the narrator never bothers to find out his name. To be so full of self-importance and to be so absolutely anonymous is irony indeed!

The Clerk (lines 285-308)

We now meet Chaucer's second touchstone character, a student taking holy orders at Oxford. To modern taste, the Clerk may seem a shade too pure, naïve and quaint, and it is sometimes suggested that Chaucer is gently poking fun at his unswerving commitment to the world of books. He and his horse are equally thin, and there is perhaps a sugges-tion that he takes advantage of his friends in order to supply himself with books:

> But al that he mighte of his freendes hente,
> On bookes and on lerninge he it spente.

However, it seems more likely that this gaunt and earnest student represents the pure search for knowledge, unadulterated by the diversions of the world and the pursuit of money. In contrast to the characters who surround him, there is no false front. He is exactly what he appears:

> Noght o word spak he moore than was neede,
> And that was seyd in forme and reverence,
> And short and quik and ful of hy sentence;
> Sowninge in moral vertu was his speche,
> And gladly wolde he lerne and gladly teche.

Just as the Knight demonstrates the Christian virtues in chivalry, so the Clerk embodies the Christian virtues in learning. We see the same self-denial in the service of a higher cause. In contrast to the Merchant, the Clerk speaks as little as possible, and, when he does speak, his words are full of that much-praised medieval quality, 'sentence', meaning 'weighty significance'. Whatever is quaint in Chaucer's description of this man, his threadbare coat, hollow cheeks and skinny horse, the Clerk's unworldliness is redeemed, if ever it needs to be redeemed, by the last line: 'And gladly wolde he lerne and gladly teche'. You could not have a more succinct exposition of the two-way process of learning.

Chaucer uses the appearance of the Clerk as an effective contrast to characters like the Monk, who is a 'lord ful fat and in good point' and whose horse is 'in greet estaat'. His threadbare clothes stand out against the 'double worstede' of the Friar and the 'sangwin and pers' of the Doctor of Physic. Unlike the other learned gentlemen in the pilgrimage the Clerk has 'but litel gold in cofre'. In contrast again to the Monk, he heeds the voice of authority in his studies 'of Aristotle and his philosophie', and his Christian concern in praying for the souls of those who finance his studies shows a truer sense of spiritual values than the Monk's 'How shal the world be served?'.

The openness and selflessness of this character throw into relief the deceptive behaviour of the Merchant and the Sergeant of the Law, the excessive indulgence of the Franklin, the pretentious concerns of the Guildsmen and the financial exploitation of knowledge practised by the Doctor of Physic. We tend nowadays to worship individuality and admire 'characters', but Chaucer would probably disagree profoundly. The egocentrics who think the world revolves entirely around them are targets in *The General Prologue*. Those who subordinate themselves to what they have to do are the centres of approval.

The Sergeant of the Law (lines 309-30)

If ever there was a focus of the different attractions in a study of Chaucer it is to be found in this character. Those interested in history can use the portrait as a marvellous insight into the legal system of the time:

> Justice he was ful often in assise,
> By patente and by pleyn commissioun.
> For his science and for his heigh renoun,
> Of fees and robes hadde he many oon.
> So greet a purchasour was nowheer noon:
> Al was fee simple to him in effect;
> His purchasing mighte nat been infect.

A 'justice in assise' is the equivalent of our circuit judge. In Chaucer's day, this would make the Sergeant among the top twenty of the legal profession of the time. He held his office both by 'patente', letters-patent from the king appointing him as a judge, and by 'pleyn commissioun', an enabling letter giving him power to exercise judgement on a wide range of offences. 'Science' has the idea of knowledge and expertise. 'Of fees and robes' is a dangerous little phrase. It might suggest that grateful clients kept the Sergeant in money and clothes. In fact, it is a reference to the legal expression *foeda et robae*. This means that the Sergeant was paid retaining fees and was in the livery of several great men for whom he would perform the occasional piece of useful legal business. A 'purchasour' is a buyer of land. We do not know whether this would be for himself or for his clients. As it is mentioned immediately after the reference to his retainers from clients, it is probably the latter. However, were it to refer to buying land for himself, this would certainly fit the Sergeant neatly into the group of professionals in the pilgrimage who are lining their own pockets and climbing through the social strata towards the status of landed gentry. This social movement is perhaps indicative of the break-up of the feudal system. Land purchase was easy money and such was his skill, he managed to secure unrestricted rights and absolute possession ('fee simple'). Chaucer has filled our heads with the Sergeant's legal jargon, so exposing the pontificating nature of this character.

Students interested in Chaucer's biographical details might wonder whether such terminology indicates legal training on Chaucer's part and also whether there is anything worth pursuing in the possible pun: 'Ther koude no wight pinche at his writing'. As a writ for Chaucer's arrest for a small debt was once signed by Thomas Pynchbek, a Sergeant of the Law, it may be that this line contains a pun and that the whole portrait is in some way a satire on Pynchbek himself.

Finally, students interested in Chaucer's use of language might examine how skilfully he controls our responses to the Sergeant:

> In termes hadde he caas and doomes alle
> That from the time of king William were falle.
> Thereto he koude endite, and make a thing.

The Sergeant surrounds himself with impressive judgements and precedents from the time of the Norman Conquest in 1066 and yet all this knowledge and skill in drawing up documents merely produces a 'thing' – the choice of word serves to devalue the Sergeant's achievement. A similar process also appears in two places where the Sergeant is first praised, and then undermined:

> Discreet he was and of greet reverence –
> He semed swich, his wordes weren so wise.

and

> Nowher so bisy a man as he ther nas,
> And yet he semed bisier than he was.

The medievalists who see the entire *Canterbury Tales* as a moral and spiritual journey will see how these quotations suggest in the Sergeant the gap between what one appears to be and what one is – perhaps the key to the characterisation.

The Franklin (lines 331–60)

The Franklin, a medieval forerunner to the country squire, is one of the more elusive characters to catch. To our eyes, he can seem a Falstaffian figure of vitality and generosity of spirit:

> Withoute bake mete was nevere his hous
> Of fissh and flessh, and that so plentevous,
> It snewed in his hous of mete and drinke,
> Of alle deyntees that men koude thinke.

However, just as modern perspectives on Falstaff may create a seriously unbalanced picture of Shakespeare's play, so we may miss much of Chaucer's pointed comment if we interpret this character too generously. In his work, Chaucer is often critical of worldly happiness and there is a considerable sense of the Franklin's misdirection in the description:

> To liven in delit was evere his wone,
> For he was Epicurus owene sone,
> That heeld opinioun that pleyn delit
> Was verray felicitee parfit.

There may also be some petulance in the Franklin's criticism of his cook for not making sharp sauces to stimulate his jaded appetite. The major criticism is implied: his pursuit of gluttonous living leaves no space for more spiritual aims.

It would be unwise, though, to miss the characteristic energy with which the Franklin celebrates the richness and open hospitality of his lifestyle. He is of a sanguine 'complexioun'; such types were red-faced, easy-going and cheerful: 'Wel loved he by the morwe a sop in wyn'. With his beard as white 'as is the dayesie' and his table 'redy covered al the longe day' it would be easy to see him as a jovial and open-handed country squire. He is described as a 'vavasour', which suggests consider-able holdings of land, and like Chaucer he was a Member of Parliament. However, compared with the strenuous Knight, dedicated to serving his faith, the Franklin lives a life dedicated only to indulgence. He may seem a more affable companion than many on the pilgrimage, but only in a worldly sense. Chaucer's audience might well recognise the excess in the Franklin's determination to 'liven in delit'. It has been suggested that the five guildsmen who follow were later additions by Chaucer to the pilgrims, and that the Cook was originally consigned to the Franklin. Bearing in mind the Cook's standards of hygiene, such a connection would place even more significantly an audience's attitude to the Franklin.

The Five Guildsmen (lines 361–78)
These five pilgrims belong to different trades but they wear the livery of a single 'solempne and. . .greet fraternitee', a social and religious guild which would protect their well-being. Chaucer uses them as an opportunity to tease the *nouveaux riches*, with their social aspirations and self-conscious taste. They blatantly wear their livery like badges of status, and are at pains to make the world aware of their possessions and income:

> Ful fressh and newe hir geere apiked was;
> Hir knives were chaped noght with bras
> But al with silver.

Like so many others, they are concerned with appearance, and Chaucer stresses this with one of his favourite words, 'semed': 'Wel semed ech of hem a fair burgeys'. There is a lovely double-edged compliment which shows scant regard for the intelligence of aldermen in:

> Everich, for the wisdom that he kan,
> Was shaply for to been an alderman.

Chaucer also stresses the aggressive greed for social priority demanded by their wives, dominating the domestic lives of these self-important public figures. We see here Chaucer again using the naïve narrator to endorse their activities:

> And elles certeyn were they to blame.
> It is ful fair to been ycleped 'madame',
> And goon to vigilies al bifore,
> And have a mantel roialliche ybore.

Their determination to take precedence at religious services is comparable to the Wife of Bath's. It is also worth pausing to note the exact effect which Chaucer achieves with the use of the word 'roialliche'. Whereas the Prioress's pretensions to 'countrefete cheere of court' are mildly amusing, the social gap between these ladies and royalty makes their aspirations openly ridiculous.

The Cook (lines 379–87)

Perhaps as a mark of status, the Guildsmen have brought their own cook with them. There is no doubt of his professional competence:

> He koude rooste, and sethe, and broille, and frie,
> Maken mortreux, and wel bake a pie,

but Chaucer here, and in the prologue to 'The Cook's Tale', shows that he is unhygienic and unscrupulous. We see his scabby, suppurating 'mormal' which he scratches while preparing all those delicacies, and in his prologue he is accused of selling pies that have been 'twies hoot and twies coold'. It is also hinted that he is a drunkard: 'Wel koude he knowe a draughte of Londoun ale'. The food he produces may look extremely attractive, but one wonders, knowing what Chaucer tells us about him, whether anyone could eat it. In this way the Cook becomes the epitome of all the characters around him. Apart from the Clerk, who exists as a touchstone to them, they are all 'seemers'. They create an image of themselves which is at variance with the reality. The Cook is the ultimate in the art of concocting: 'For blankmanger, that made he with the beste'.

In the 'Pardoner's Tale', cooks are criticised as agents of gluttony, who 'turnen substaunce into accident', and people like the Franklin who indulge in the sin are damned:

> But, certes, he that haunteth swich delices
> Is deed, whil that he lyveth in tho vices.

One is often aware of a tension in Chaucer between an attitude and judgements that celebrate this world with its rich fabric and variety, and an awareness of ultimate judgement which consigns those whose lives do not approach prescribed patterns to purgation and possible damnation. We may appreciate the pilgrims' vitality without forgetting their ultimate destiny.

The Shipman (lines 388–410)

Chaucer's Shipman seems to have been based on a real person; certainly there was a boat called the 'Magdaleyne' sailing from Dartmouth between 1379 and 1391. The Dartmouth ships at that time were frequently charged with attacking Breton fishing boats, and from a study of the records it is almost possible to identify the Shipman as a certain Peter Risshenden. Chaucer has delightfully caught this man, so proficient as a seaman, so inept on a horse: 'He rood upon a rouncy as he kouthe', and who wore his dagger, seaman-fashion, hanging from a cord round his neck so that he could keep both hands free.

The Shipman can be balanced against the Yeoman. Both are deeply tanned by the elements and are craftsmen in their way, the essential difference being the quiet competence of the Yeoman and the blatant lack of scruple shown by the Shipman: 'Of nice conscience took he no keep'. The narrator describes him as a 'good felawe', though ironically his 'goodness' consists of draining wine from casks in transit while merchants slept off their seasickness, and callously drowning any prisoners captured in sea-fights, as revealed in the euphemistic line: 'By water he sente hem hoom to every lond'. Nonetheless, there is some balance of attitudes here. The narrator recognises the strength of character and the navigational skills required to survive at sea:

> But of his craft to rekene wel his tides,
> His stremes, and his daungers him bisides,
> His herberwe, and his moone, his lodemenage,

> Ther nas noon swich from Hulle to Cartage.
> Hardy he was and wys to undertake;
> With many a tempest hadde his berd been shake.

We should not be too surprised at the cruelty so casually indicated in the portrait. Edward III, the king for much of Chaucer's life, could initiate a Round Table for chivalric knights and found the Order of the Garter in 1344, for the noblest Knights in the nation; at the same time, he would have slaughtered the Burghers of Calais had it not been for the sympathy of his wife, Queen Philippa. Despite the ideals enshrined in stories, and even in *The General Prologue* itself, real life was predominantly brutal with those vanquished in battle, unless they were a marketable commodity and could be ransomed – as Chaucer himself was in 1360.

Chaucer has drawn his pilgrims from all over southern England. The Shipman and the Wife of Bath have travelled from the west, the Reeve from Norfolk. The Sergeant of the Law and the Franklin appear to live somewhere in the Home Counties, while the Merchant seems to operate from near Ipswich. Others are specifically from London. In line with Chaucer's inclusive vision there is in the pilgrimage a variety of origin as well as a mixing in terms of social position and moral attitudes, and this specificness helps to add realism to his work.

The Doctor of Physic (lines 411–44)

Like many of the professional class among the pilgrims, the Doctor is extremely proficient in his work, and highly dubious in moral and spiritual matters. Rich, well-dressed and knowledgeable within the terms of medieval medicine, the Doctor is dedicated to money:

> He kepte that he wan in pestilence.
> For gold in phisik is a cordial,
> Therefore he lovede gold in special.

Chaucer's England had several visits from the plague – the Black Death. During his lifetime, the population was reduced from a probable three millions to two millions. There would be deserted villages scattered through the landscape. Imminent death was an ever-present fact of life, and here is this irreligious physician coining money from sickness and lining his own and the chemists' pockets from the suffering. While the Franklin may be somewhat redeemed by his generosity, the abstemious Doctor is a tight-fisted old Scrooge: 'And yet he was but esy of dispence'.

He might further be contrasted with the threadbare Clerk whose pure quest for knowledge, close study of the Bible and generosity of spirit, 'And gladly wolde he lerne and gladly teche', are in marked opposition to the mercenary aims and scant Biblical knowledge of the Doctor: 'His studie was but litel on the Bible'.

He is in a way similar to the Shipman. Both show little regard for others, but there is a coldness about the Doctor, as he goes about enriching himself behind his professional mask, that makes him offensive in a way that the Shipman never is. Finally, there is the major irony implied by the verbal echo of the Knight: 'He was a verray, parfit praktisour'.

We learn a great deal about medieval medicinal practice from this portrait:

> He kepte his pacient a ful greet deel
> In houres by his magik natureel.
> Wel koude he fortunen the ascendent
> Of his images for his pacient.
> He knew the cause of everich maladie,
> Were it of hoot, or coold, or moist, or drie,
> And where they engendred, and of what humour.

We see the importance of choosing the most astrologically auspicious time for starting any treatment. The prognosis was enhanced by making charms engraved with astrological symbols or even with images of the patient. Diagnosis was often an assessment of the balance between the four elemental qualities: hot, cold, moist and dry. More is said about the humours in section 1.2.

The Wife of Bath (lines 445-76)

There are major disagreements about this character. Many modern readers will see, in her lively challenge to established attitudes, an early representative of Women's Liberation, and many who find images of perfection uncomfortable will find her more attractive than the unworldly Clerk. Moreover, she has lived! There is a vitality and a sense of adventure about her. She has been given by Chaucer a will and energy, regardless of religious intent, to travel to Jerusalem three times, as well as visiting Rome and Northern Spain. While some may see in her knowledge of remedies of love a suggestion of skills in abortion, others will argue that the phrase may refer to nothing more than mending broken hearts, or at the worst, the making of love-potions and aphrodisiacs to smooth the path of love.

She could be interpreted as a ferocious monument to the destructive nature of acquisitive sexual demands. She has killed off five husbands through her voracious appetites: 'Withouten oother compaignie in youthe!' With her sharp spurs, 'gat'-teeth and scarlet stockings, she would probably strike fear rather than admiration in the hearts of all but the strongest men.

Interestingly, medieval physiognomists might well agree with Freudian commentators over some of the details in the characterisation. There was a readily available system of physiognomy which interpreted facial and other details as reflections of the inner person. Hence the red face and the spiky teeth would be associated with a strongly lascivious temperament. A similar conclusion might be drawn today from the Freudian implications of her 'spores sharpe'.

When we look at the portrait, we first notice her deafness. We are later informed in the *Prologue* to her tale that this was caused by her fifth husband, who clouted her to the ground when she tore out a page from a book he was reading. It is a marvellous piece of realistic detail. She was annoyed at Jankin, her husband, having quoted at her a stream of tales about wicked wives and dangerous women, and so she petulantly ripped three pages out.

In this portrait, her deafness is part of her loudness. We can imagine her on the pilgrimage, the only woman apart from the fastidious Prioress, with whom she would have little in common, laughing and carping with the men and shouting to hear the sound of her own voice. We do not know whether it is only in her own estimation that her skill in weaving surpasses that of the Flemish weavers, or whether the narrator is genuinely giving credit where it is due. It is clear through that the pique which led to her deafness is also the cause of her anger when anyone dared to claim precedence over her as she went up to make an offering in church. This situation was a stock illustration in medieval times for the sin of Pride, and it may be that Chaucer wants us to see both the deafness and the anger as something more than physical description. Perhaps it is the deafness of one who wilfully will not hear the voice of authority, and the anger, too, may show how close the Wife is to mortal sin. Whether Chaucer wants us to react with humour at the picture of the outraged harridan or whether we are to consider the implications of her pride is uncertain, but there is no doubt that we are to smile as we see her balancing her Sunday finery on her head with a steadfastness of purpose known only to the truly dedicated follower of fashion! The aggressive flamboyance shown in the ten-pound headscarf is further stressed by her red stockings which match her bold red face, and her huge hat: 'As brood as is a bokeler or a targe.' Everything about this woman is larger than life – her voice, her sexual experience and her taste in clothes. In one way this suggests coarseness and vulgarity, but along with these there exists a vitality and a passion for experience.

The Wife was much travelled, and in this way may be compared with the Knight and contrasted with the Parson. The Knight travels out of a sense of service, 'in his lordes werre'. Dame Alisoun, the Wife, travels the routes to the main places of pilgrimage more for diversion than for religious reasons. The Parson does not travel beyond the confines of his parish, but every step he makes has a purpose whereas the Wife'... koude muchel of wandringe by the weye'. The ambiguity of the line makes the point, through its pun on the word 'wandringe'.

The Parson (lines 477-528)
Following the complex characterisation of the Wife of Bath, there are two significantly placed touchstone pilgrims, the Parson and the Plowman. If you look at the seemingly random assortment of pilgrims on the journey to Canterbury, you will find various patterns of significance. There is, of course, the social grouping that extends from the Knight to the Plowman. There is also a moral framework that would put the Knight and the Plowman together close to the top. Some characters are paired, either as travelling companions like the Sergeant of the Law and the Franklin, the Summoner and the Pardoner and the Parson and the Plowman, or, like the Miller and the Reeve and the Prioress and the Wife of Bath, paired as opposites. There is a much more subtle organisation which relates the pilgrims in dynamic groups with each other. The Knight's party appropriately starts the *Prologue* because the Knight is the most socially important pilgrim. He can also set an appropriate moral tone. However, his group immediately and naturally breaks up the hierarchical straight-jacket by the inclusion of the Yeoman. The integrity of this group is balanced by the deviation from duty of the next three pilgrims, the Prioress, Monk and Friar. Then follows a large group comprising, with the significant exception of the Clerk, a range of the new professionals who are very often interested only in the external values of life. Chaucer now places against this group two 'brothers', the Parson and the Plowman, who base their lives entirely on the precepts of their faith. The sterling qualities of these two are also carried forward and significantly place the final

sweepings of the pilgrimage, the rogues' gallery that delightfully includes the narrator himself.

There are other patterns, of course. *The General Prologue* is a mine of significant balances and relationships. The Church is the largest single organisation represented on the pilgrimage, with six of the major characters in its employ. They produce a range of reaction from gentle amusement to outraged disgust. At their centre, radiating the ultimate in Christian duty, is the Parson:

> He waited after no pompe and reverence,
> Ne maked him a spiced conscience,
> But Cristes loore and his apostles twelve
> He taughte, but first he folwed it himselve.

The Parson is everything the other clerics are not. He fulfils himself through his duty to his flock. He is not the slightest bit interested in advancement or money:

> He sette nat his benefice to hire
> And leet his sheep encombed in the mire
> And ran to Londoun unto Seinte Poules
> To seken him a chaunterie for soules,
> Or with a bretherhed to been withholde;
> But dwelte at hoom, and kepte wel his folde,
> So that the wolf ne made it nat miscarie;
> He was a shepherde and noght a mercenarie.

The last line expresses the basic difference between the Parson and many on the pilgrimage. The shepherd concept, with its suggestions of Christ the Shepherd and His self-sacrifice for mankind, is of the same nature as the Knight's surrender of self to his faith, the Clerk's devotion to learning and the Plowman's selfless practical love for his neighbour. All the other characters are in love either with themselves or with money. The Parson may be poor in the world's opinion but he is rich in spiritual virtue. The central thrust of the character is that he teaches by example. There is no separation between what he says and what he does: 'That first he wroghte, and afterward he taughte'.

When you examine the virtues of this priest you will see that there is something of the Lollard in his style of administering the Gospel. The Lollards were the followers of Wycliffe, who spoke out strongly against the abuses of the Church. Wycliffe operated very much under the patronage of John of Gaunt, with whose household Chaucer had close connections. Chaucer also had several friends who were strongly influenced by Lollard ideals, though there is no evidence that Chaucer was actively associated with the sect. However, Chaucer's attacks on the corrupt practices and worldly bias of the institutionalised Church do reveal some sympathy with Wycliffe's ideas:

> Wel oghte a preest ensample for to yive,
> By his clennesse, how that his sheep sholde live.

The Parson strenuously avoids the seductions of easy money singing for departed souls or accepting retainers from rich guilds or fraternities. Instead, he practises Christ's precepts and jealously watches over his parishioners. But while he is good, he is no doormat:

> But. . .were any persone obstinat,
> What so he were, of heigh or lough estat,
> Him wolde he snibben sharply for the nonis.

You cannot imagine the Friar behaving like that!

This character appears to be the moral heart of the poem. His behaviour offers important perspectives on other pilgrims and his tale is the penitential point towards which they journey. Many of the other travellers are obliquely and damningly referred to in his tale, particularly in the catalogue of the Seven Deadly Sins. Of course, implicit in all the judgements is the possibility of last-minute penitence, literally whilst falling from the stirrup to the ground, so not all those most enveloped in sin would be necessarily doomed. However, it is a sobering thought that many of the characters most appealing to modern taste are those who, in the Parson's eyes, deserve most 'to be snibben sharply for the nonis'.

The Plowman (lines 529–41)

In the same way that the Parson acts as the model of perfection for the clerical pilgrims, the Plowman is the model of the perfect Christian to compare with the secular members of the company. He is aptly described as the Parson's brother, whether this is meant literally or metaphorically. He completes the idealised representation of the four estates. The Knight as a noble loved 'chivalrie, trouthe and honour, fredom and curteisie'. The Clerk 'of studie took. . .moost cure and most heede'. The Parson 'Cristes gospel trewely wolde preche'. And now the Plowman, as the representative of the peasantry on whom the stability of the nation depended, appears as the true labourer for God:

> A trewe swinkere and a good was he,
> Livinge in pees and parfit charitee.
> God loved he best with al his hoole herte
> At alle times, thogh him gamed or smerte,
> And thanne his neighebor right as himselve.

With the social and political unrest prevalent in the latter part of the fourteenth century, and particularly remembering the Peasants' Revolt of 1381, the portrait might be suggesting a wish that all peasants were as piously motivated as the Plowman.

The real strength of the portrayal, however, lies in its universal Christian symbolism; although it opens with a strongly unsentimental comment that the man 'hadde ylad of dong ful many a fother', the rest of the description is almost entirely a collection of precepts, expressing an ideal pattern for a humble existence, at least to medieval minds: hard, honest work, a generosity of spirit and a close approximation of life to Holy Writ. One senses that implicit in the portrait is what most peasants of the time were not doing, namely working for charity rather than profit and paying their tithes appropriately without any sense of grudge. The most significant phrase of all is 'parfit charitee', with its plain reminder of the Wife of Bath's failing in that direction.

Chaucer seems to pause to regroup after his description of the Parson and the Plowman, and this pause helps to lay emphasis on them. They stand together, like beacons, powerfully illuminating the landscape around them, with their integrity throwing into strong relief the 'seemers' who precede them and the cheats and graspers who follow. This last group contains some of the most sharply-drawn of all the pilgrims, and the most unlikeable, together with the most elusive, Chaucer's narrator.

The Miller (lines 545-66)

This is a robustly orchestrated characterisation, full of seemingly individual physical and symbolic touches. The Miller is a one-man noise machine. He is aggressive, running at doors and smashing them with his head; he is a great wrestler, full of coarse jokes, with a mouth like a furnace, and plays the Devil's instrument, the bagpipe. Like the others around him in this last group, he is a cheat: 'Wel koude he stelen corn and tollen thries'. When we look at the details of the portrait we become aware that, although Chaucer's audience and a modern reader would probably agree about the nature of the Miller, they would have arrived at similar conclusions from differing interpretations of the evidence:

His berd as any sowe or fox was reed,
And therto brood, as though it were a spade.
Upon the cop right of his nose he hade
A werte, and theron stood a toft of heris,
Reed as the brustles of a sowes eris;
His nosethirles blake were and wide.
A swerd and bokeler bar he by his side.
His mouth as greet was as a greet forneys.

The medieval listeners would pick up clues from the Miller's red spade beard, his flattened nose with its wide nostrils, the wart on top of that nose and the mouth gaping like a furnace, and deduce from these that the Miller was an aggressive, argumentative and lecherous type. Chaucer's audience might well be reminded of fiendish gargoyles and would certainly connect the Miller's huge mouth, and the fact that he played the bagpipe, with the work of the Devil, the mouth in particular representing the gateway to Hell. What issued from it was the product of the fires of Hell, the work of Satan to subvert mankind.

The modern reader does not operate with the same sense of reference. The details that place the Miller as a type to a medieval, shape him as an individual to us. What emerges is his brute energy, the edgy danger lurking just below the surface, the association with sows, notorious for their unpredictability, and foxes, noted for their cunning.

Chaucer shows a lively awareness throughout *The General Prologue* of the cheats, frauds and fiddles practised in his time. The Miller's particular technique is to claim three times his due of flour from his customers for grinding their corn. Like all millers, according to tradition, he was dishonest: the way he sampled corn with his thumb had made him rich.

The Manciple (lines 567–86)

Perhaps one reason why the Miller seems so sharply individualised is that he is placed between two shadowy characters. The Plowman emerges as having great strength of character, but we know little about his appearance. The Manciple, similarly, is described entirely through his deeds. A manciple was a servant who bought provisions for a college at university or an inn of court which would accommodate lawyers. No one emerges with much credit from this tart little portrait. The lawyers, the 'heep of lerned men' who employ this 'lewed' manciple, are cheated by him easily and profitably. The tone of the portrait is not sufficiently comic for us to celebrate the triumph of the native wit of the shady manciple over the refined intelligence of the thirty or so lawyers, 'That weren of lawe expert and curious'. Instead, the narrator comments with pointed irony:

> Now is nat that of God a ful fair grace
> That swich a lewed mannes wit shal pace
> The wisdom of an heep of lerned men?

We are beginning to sense that there is a new spirit abroad, which Chaucer does not find congenial – a spirit of competitiveness for wealth clearly demonstrated by so many of the new professional class among the pilgrims. It is almost as though Chaucer is regretting that, for many, the ideal is no longer honour, but money. As an early fifteenth-century rhyme says:

> Man upon mold, whatsoever thou be,
> I warn utterly thou getyst no degre,
> Ne no worshyp abyd with the,
> But* thou have the peny redy to tak to.
>
> *But = unless

Chaucer's rogues all seem to have 'the peny redy'!

The Reeve (lines 587–622)
In contrast to the Manciple, the Reeve, an estate manager, is very clearly delineated:

> The Reve was a sclendre colerik man.
> His berd was shave as ny as ever he kan;
> His heer was by his eris ful round yshorn;
> His top was dokked lyk a preest biforn.
> Ful longe were his legges and ful lene,
> Ylik a staf, ther was no calf ysene.
> Wel koude he kepe a gerner and a binne;
> Ther was noon auditour koude on him winne.

All the details of the Reeve's appearance are those regularly associated by physiognomists with a testy and choleric nature, so to that extent he is a typical character. However, because he is given a particular place to live, near Baldeswelle in Norfolk, and a named horse to ride, Scot, there is some sense of an individual in the portrait. Perhaps it gives him some perverse pleasure to be so lowly and to be so rich? Perhaps in his mean-minded, ascetic way, he cannot bear to be associated personally with anything luxurious, so he wears his hair trimmed and his beard 'shave as ny as ever he kan'.

While the long, lean legs may belong to traditional descriptions and further illustrate the 'sclendre colerik' type who burns up all his energies to feed his temperament, the simple 'Ylik a staf' and its subsequent descriptive qualification, 'ther was no calf ysene', tilts the characterisation into humour. There is, after all, something ridiculous in such self-consuming malevolence. What is more, the Reeve is set up to perform an embittered double-act with the Miller, to whom he forms the perfect visual and temperamental opposite. Where the Miller is aggressively gregarious and leads the pilgrims out of London, playing his infernal bagpipes, the Reeve rides last, creating around him an atmosphere of bleak social isolation. We can see the effect he has on others by the reaction he evokes from subordinates with whom he has dealings: 'They were adrad of him as of the deeth'.

Like the Miller and the Manciple, he is an eminently successful cheater of those he should serve. The Reeve seems to be somewhere between a steward and a bailiff in his management of his lord's estates. In fact, such is his skill that the whole estate: 'Was hoolly in this Reves governinge'. It seems to have been a matter of sour pride that, to any outside observer, he is meticulous at his work. His accounts balance so that no auditor can spot any embezzlement, the bills are paid promptly and he knows all the dodges that might be practised by the workmen. The ultimate triumph is to lend to the master what in fact already belongs to him, and for the Reeve to receive in return thanks, accommodation and clothing.

His meticulous cheating has brought him riches and a fine house, appropriately hidden away, but the man carries around with him his own personal winter and a rusty sword, possibly a pointed metaphor for the decline of chivalry, and certainly an indication that this man does not achieve success through honourable means.

The Summoner (lines 623–68)

Just as the Parson and Plowman are two linked brothers in virtue, so the last two pilgrims are linked brothers in sin. These two Antichrist figures, cynical dispensers of perversions of sacred justice and sacred mercy, bring us closer to horrific visions of judgement and the nightmare world of lost souls. At the same time, they have something about them of the fascination of the grotesque in children's stories and the charged delight that sometimes sparks from a contemplation of horror. Regardless of their moral impact, artistically the portraits are a triumph. Chaucer has caught the rogues exquisitely and balanced their relationship in all kinds of telling ways.

A summoner was, exactly as his name suggests, someone appointed to call to ecclesiastical courts those who had transgressed against the laws of the Church. It was a post that offered considerable scope for corruption and the abuse of power, opportunities eagerly exploited by this particular summoner and many others of his calling.

We see straight away that the Summoner's face reflects an inner chaos and torment of a different order from the physical details and sores that we have met in previous pilgrims. We note his 'fyr-reed cherubinnes face' and pick up the associations of hellfire; we wonder whether the reference to cherubim is heavy irony, that one so damned should be described in such heavenly terms, or whether the cherubim, traditionally associated with red faces, are part of some apocalyptic vision. The chaos within is breaking down the surface of his skin in a form of leprosy and forcing through the flesh in the form of boils and carbuncles on his cheeks. With his narrow eyes, sparse beard and scabby eyebrows, every physical detail about the Summoner is disgusting. The narrator states bluntly: 'Of his visage children were aferd'. When we remember that children are traditionally closest to God, the state of this man's soul becomes all too apparent. His buffoonery and ignorance, his drunkenness and sexual proclivities make him even more revolting, but we have not yet touched on the central criticism of the Summoner, his abuse of office.

The Summoner rides, ridiculously garlanded and with a cake, presumably taken from some tavern, as a shield. Chaucer's narrator, who has been allowing the descriptions of the characters to speak for themselves for some time, is forced to react to this monster. He points the ignorance of the Summoner who when drunk will speak only Latin:

> A few termes hadde he, two or thre,
> That he had lerned out of som decree -
> No wonder is, he herde it al the day;
> And eek ye knowen wel how that a jay
> Kan clepen 'Watte' as wel as kan the pope.

The narrator is even moved to open rebuke, the only time in *The General Prologue*, when he describes the disgraceful exploitation by the Summoner of his function. Having condoned, 'for a quart of wyn', a priest's keeping a mistress, the Summoner suggests that any offender might avoid prison and excommunication by paying a large fine, presumably including a substantial fee for his services. This provokes the strong reaction from the narrator, who accuses the Summoner of a downright lie:

> Of cursing oghte ech gilty man him drede,
> For curs wol slee right as assoilling savith,
> And also war him of a 'Significavit'.

Perhaps the narrator protests too much, and his somewhat naïve sense of outrage stresses rather than diminishes the venality of such courts and their servants.

The Summoner is 'hoot' and 'lecherous as a sparwe' and 'a finch eek koude he pulle' when so inclined, but he is also enmeshed in a homosexual relationship with the Pardoner. There is something distinctly chilling in the fact that this hideous monster had all the young people in the diocese at his mercy. 'Girles' means both men and women. The mind boggles at the kind of corrupting advice he might offer them, and this lends a venomous irony to the narrator's seeming pleasantry:

> He was a gentil harlot and a kinde;
> A bettre felawe sholde men noght finde.

Chaucer's scathing satire seems to reach a new intensity in this portrait.

The Pardoner (lines 669–714)

Accompanying the Summoner is his special friend, the Pardoner. They are linked in song as well as in sin. We respond to the scene with a complex pattern of emotions. It is both amusing and shocking, repulsive and fascinating as the ridiculous but dangerous pair sing a love duet, the Summoner in a deep bass, the Pardoner in a bleating alto.

The details of the Pardoner's description are repelling. His hair as yellow as wax hanging in thin and greasy rats' tails, and his sadly ridiculous pretensions to travelling in the latest fashion, prepare us, but not sufficiently to entirely eliminate a sense of shock, for the enormity of the impact and the predicament of this character. When we learn of his practices it is as though we have suddenly found ourselves sitting in church and watching Dr Goebbels, Adolf Hitler's venomous propagandist in the Second World War, climbing the steps to the pulpit. The Pardoner, with his glaring eyes and sexual ambivalence, is spitting out his venom and disguising it as holiness, taking revenge on the innocent for the deficiencies in his physical make-up.

Though he may be repulsive, he has power and he is brutally effective:

> But of his craft, fro Berwik into Ware,
> Ne was ther swich another pardoner.

Pardoners were sellers of Papal indulgences, whereby a sinner could gain remission from penance in exchange for a cash payment. In the fourteenth century their practices came increasingly under criticism, and the hostel of Rouncivale, near Charing Cross in London, was notorious for condoning the unauthorised sale of pardons. We notice the devastating giveaway of our Pardoner's techniques – a pillow case which he claims is the veil of the Virgin Mary, pigs' bones masquerading as those of a saint, chunks of sail and a cheap cross – but with these, and:

> . . . with feyned flaterie and japes,
> He made the person and the peple his apes.

The ultimate irony is that so loathsome and immoral a creature should be so supremely convincing in church:

> But trewely to tellen atte laste,
> He was in chirche a noble ecclesiaste.
> Wel koude he rede a lessoun or a storie,
> But alderbest he song an offertorie;
> For wel he wiste, whan that song was songe,
> He moste preche and wel affile his tonge
> To winne silver, as he ful wel koude;
> Therefore he song the murierly and loude.

Chaucer, the supreme artist, has created another artist of supreme skill. There is no doubt that, from a technical point of view, the Pardoner is a craftsman of the first order, but all his craft is dedicated to winning silver and therefore misdirected. When he finishes his tale to the pilgrims, he admits that Christ's pardon is the ultimate and he would not deceive his travelling companions. The irony is that, if he believes in Divine Judgement and Christ's pardon, he must know that of all the souls to whom he cynically offers fake salvation, he is the one most in need. And yet, perversely, he must obsessively practise the skills that ensure his own damnation. Hence, his singing 'the murierly and loude' hangs in the air with the awful implications of a transient triumph in the face of ultimate judgement and doom.

There seems little doubt that from an artistic point of view Chaucer enjoys his rogues and grotesques. However, the skill with which he presents them should not blind us to the fact that 'Al that is writen is writen for oure doctrine', and that while there were excesses and corruption in the institutions of the Church, its fundamental teachings were unchallenged. Human experience was framed by birth and death and after death came judgement. Chaucer's pilgrims should ultimately be seen in the light of their accountability to their status and employment. Hence, many of the assessments, regardless of the fun the characters offer, will be of a moral nature. But to be moral, as Chaucer shows, is not to be dull.

The Apology (lines 725–46)

To some extent, this is a traditional medieval expression of artistic unworthiness or a request for some kind of sympathetic understanding for the author from his audience. Chaucer uses it frequently. It is, up to a point, a mere convention, but it does bring to the audience the idea of the narrator as a particular character, seeming to cope with the problem of the various linguistic styles of the pilgrims, and inviting the audience to consider as real the words spoken by the tellers of the tales:

> For this ye knowen al so wel as I,
> Whoso shal telle a tale after a man,
> He moot reherce as ny as evere he kan
> Everich a word, if it be in his charge,
> Al speke he never so rudeliche and large,
> Or ellis he moot telle his tale untrewe,
> Or feyne thing, or finde wordes newe.

This is perhaps a major artistic achievement of *The Canterbury Tales*. While so many of the ideas and the feeling of the work remain rooted in a medieval culture, that sense of voice, separate for each character, and that individuality of conscience is the beginning of something new. The stories become dramatic extensions of the characters portrayed in *The General Prologue* and the linking passages between the tales are filled with a sense of realistic social interchange. Characters are being set in specific situations and realistic clashes of personality intrude on the more formalised pattern of relationships that are found in *The General Prologue*.

The Host (lines 747–821)

His is one voice we do hear directly in *The General Prologue*. Apart from the Summoner's: 'Purs is the ercedekenes helle,' his drunken *Questio quid iuris* and a snatch of song, Chaucer uses the narrator to report what he has gleaned from the other travellers. However, it is now appropriate for the narrator to take his place with the other pilgrims. A different kind of voice is structurally required to initiate and control the range of stories that are to follow. As the presiding genius to the whole scheme of stories, the Host should be seen in some respects as a complement to the narrator. Chaucer has created a pliancy in the character of his narrator, so that the illusion is created of other characters opening out to someone whom they see as no threat. The Host is endowed with coercive qualities. He is a robust and hearty chairman who can suggest the idea of telling stories, intervene effectively and hold the framework together. The purpose behind the characterisation is different from the others in *The General Prologue*. Chaucer is using Harry Bailly, as we later learn his name to be, as a function of the plan of *The Canterbury Tales*.

The Journey (lines 822–58)

> And forth we riden a litel moore than paas
> Unto the watering of Seint Thomas.

One of the delights of reading Chaucer is to see how much he belongs to his time, how he is rooted in the theology and values of late medieval England. At the same time we are aware of how he transcends his time. In this couplet we have both elements. The medieval mind would dwell on the physically sustaining qualities of water and then move to consider the power of its metaphorical and spiritual sustenance and cleansing. The modern mind may see the couplet as an attempt at creating an illusion of reality. Here is an actual pilgrimage, actually stopping at an actual place. With one set of perspectives we are looking for patterns of allegory, and significances that surrender their meanings from a concentration on detail; with another, we respond to characters reacting realistically to features on a landscape. We need both patterns of awareness if we are to begin to catch the richness and pleasure in Chaucer.

6 SPECIMEN PASSAGE AND CRITICAL COMMENTARY

6.1 SPECIMEN PASSAGE

The Wife of Bath (lines 445–76)

> A good WIF was ther OF biside BATHE,
> But she was somdel deef, and that was scathe.
> Of clooth-making she hadde swich an haunt,
> She passed hem of Ypres and of Gaunt.
> In al the parisshe wif ne was ther noon
> That to the offringe bifore hire sholde goon;
> And if ther dide, certeyn so wrooth was she,
> That she was out of alle charitee.
> Hir coverchiefs ful fine weren of ground;
> I dorste swere they weyeden ten pound
> That on a Sonday weren upon hir heed.
> Hir hosen weren of fyn scarlet reed,
> Ful streite yteyd, and shoes ful moiste and newe.
> Boold was hir face, and fair, and reed of hewe.
> She was a worthy womman al hir live:
> Housbondes at chirche dore she hadde five,
> Withouten oother compaignye in youthe, –
> But therof nedeth nat to speke as nowthe.
> And thries hadde she been at Jerusalem;
> She hadde passed many a straunge strem;
> At Rome she hadde been, and at Boloigne,
> In Galice at Seint-Jame, and at Coloigne.
> She koude muchel of wandringe by the weye.

Gat-tothed was she, soothly for to seye.
Upon an amblere esily she sat,
Ywimpled wel, and on hir heed an hat
As brood as is a bokeler or a targe;
A foot-mantel aboute hir hipes large,
And on hir feet a paire of spores sharpe.
In felaweshipe wel koude she laughe and carpe.
Of remedies of love she knew per chaunce,
For she koude of that art the olde daunce.

6.2 CRITICAL COMMENTARY

The basic meaning of this passage has already been discussed in the general commentary, so what we are looking at here are mainly questions of technique. Chaucer is not a writer whose technique draws attention to itself. His verse is transparent in the sense that we can read the poem without being aware of the poetic skills involved, but beneath this clarity can be seen at work a highly proficient craftsman. The strength of the poetry depends on the choice of words and the manipulation of the rhyming couplet, which combine to produce the delicate variations in tone which are so characteristic of Chaucer.

The portrait of the Wife of Bath demonstrates very clearly Chaucer's skilful use of the couplet. The portrait starts with the basic instance where the couplet forms a complete unit, and each line is also self-contained:

A good WIF was ther OF biside BATHE,
But she was somdel deef, and that was scathe.

Elsewhere Chaucer cuts across this simple form in order to achieve a variety of effects. Notice, for example, the technical skill involved in the following lines:

Hir coverchiefs ful fine weren of ground;
I dorste swere they weyeden ten pound
That on a Sonday weren upon hir heed.
His hosen weren of fyn scarlet reed,
Ful streite yteyd, and shoes ful moiste and newe.
Boold was hir face, and fair, and reed of hewe.

The objective here is to create space for the striking single line at the end, which stands out on its own and is very important in giving us an impression of the Wife. In order to do this, Chaucer prises the sense of the previous lines away from their natural rhymes. By running on from 'ten pound' into 'That on a Sonday' Chaucer breaks the rhyme scheme at 'heed'. The following two lines form a sense unit and not a rhyming unit. This then leaves the last line isolated and stresses the words 'Boold', 'fair' and 'reed'.

An even more subtle and delightful instance can be found in these lines:

> She was a worthy womman al hir live:
> Housbondes at chirche dore she hadde five,
> Withouten oother compaignye in youthe, -
> But therof nedeth nat to speke as nowthe.

Technically the first line stands on its own, and lines two and three go together. However, the rhymes 'live' and 'five' force the first two lines to interact, and make the word 'worthy' strongly ironic, as it is implied that her worthiness is dependent on her having had five husbands! This irony is further reinforced by the offhand remark about her earlier sexual adventures, and the seemingly dismissive 'But therof nedeth nat to speke as nowthe', which completes the couplet, in fact stresses the importance of the preceding comments.

This portrait, as well as showing Chaucer's skill with the couplet form, also shows his sure control over alliterative effects and other sound textures. The structure of a line, or a series of lines, can imitate what is being described:

> Upon an amblere esily she sat,
> Ywimpled wel, and on hir heed an hat
> As brood as is a bokeler or a targe.

In the first line the series of initial vowels (a legitimate form of alliteration in the Middle Ages) conveys the rhythm of a horse's gentle walking, while 'she sat' suggests emphatically the blunt physicality of the Wife's presence. When Chaucer describes her hat he makes the line flow through the constraints of the rhyme scheme to suggest in terms of sound, 'brood as is a bokeler', as well as in terms of language the spreading breadth of her huge headgear.

Other examples where alliteration is used to good effect include 'worthy womman', 'wandringe by the weye' and 'spores sharpe'. 'Worthy womman' appears to be a simple association of sounds and words, but becomes pointed when the meaning of 'worthy' is modified in the ensuing lines, as has been explained above. 'Wandringe by the weye' is a strikingly memorable phrase which invites us to ponder its ambiguity. Finally, 'spores sharpe' is almost onomatopoeic in its emphasis. Alliteration, in addition to producing poetic effects, is sometimes used just for conventional tags or line-fillers like 'soothly for to seye'.

Just as we are in danger of missing the deftness of Chaucer's poetic skills unless we pay particular attention to them, so we are also in danger of missing many points of significance that are concealed in seemingly innocent detail. Consider the second line: 'But she was somdel deef, and that was scathe.' The narrator presumably means nothing more than 'it was a pity that she was rather deaf', but we must consider whether her deafness is more than physical. If she is spiritually deaf then the tone of the phrase 'that was scathe' becomes critical rather than sympathetic. Similarly, 'she koude muchel of wandringe by the weye', when seen in moral terms, changes from a mere observation to a moral stricture.

What we have seen in this portrait can be seen throughout Chaucer's poetry, and each fresh approach to the text reveals new subtleties, meanings and insights. Chaucer is not a poet for the casual reader - he is difficult to get to know well, but the effort is worth making.

7 CRITICAL RECEPTION

The best presentations of comment on Chaucer are: *Introduction to Five Hundred Years of Chaucer Criticism and Allusion, 1357 – 1900* by Caroline Spurgeon (Cambridge University Press) and *Geoffrey Chaucer,* Penguin Critical Anthologies, edited by J. A. Burrow. We are indebted to both.

The best short commentary on Chaucerian criticism is an essay called *Images of Chaucer*. This can be found in *Chaucer and the Chaucerians*, a critical anthology edited by the writer of the essay, D. S. Brewer.

Chaucer was admired by his contemporaries for his philosophical sentiments and his skill as a translator into English from French and Italian. There is very little early written comment on *The Canterbury Tales*, until William Caxton's preface to the second edition of *The Canterbury Tales*, 'in whiche I fynde many a noble hystorye of every astate and degre, fyrst rehercyng the condicions and th'arraye of eche of them as properly as possyble is to be sayd'.

Perhaps the finest early general comment occurs anonymously in the *Book of Courtesy*, in 1477. The writer points out various aspects of Chaucer's craft and, in the last couplet, succinctly catches the essence of great writing.

> Redith his werkis, ful of plesaunce,
> Clere in sentence, in langage excellent,
> Briefly to wryte such was his suffysance
> Whatever to saye he toke to his entente
> His langage was so fayr and pertynente
> It semeth unto mannys heerynge
> Not only the worde, but verely the thynge.

Chaucer's words have never lost that power to recreate in the reader's imagination the almost physical actuality of his subject matter, whether it be the heady intoxication of a spring day, or the violent toughness of the Miller.

Chaucer's stature as a poet has not, however, always been fully respected. By the late seventeenth century Joseph Addison reflected a mood that found Chaucer quaint and not particularly amusing or appropriate morally:

> Long had our dull forefathers slept supine,
> Nor felt the raptures of the tuneful nine;
> Till Chaucer first, a merry bard, arose,
> And many a story told in rhyme and prose.
> But age has rusted what the poet writ,
> Worn out his language, and obscur'd his wit.
> In vain he jests in his unpolish'd strain
> And tries to make his readers laugh in vain.

John Dryden, a contemporary of Addison, also found Chaucer's verse 'unpolish'd':

> The verse of Chaucer, I confess, is not harmonious to us. . . they who lived with him, and some time after him, thought it musical; and it continues so even in our judgement, if compared with the numbers of Lydgate and Gower, his contemporaries: there is the rude sweetness of a Scotch tune in it, which is natural and pleasing, though not perfect.

Dryden excuses this deficiency by arguing that poetically Chaucer was a primitive. 'We can only say, that he lived in the infancy of our poetry, and that nothing is brought to perfection at the first.' This condescending tone should not prevent our recognising that Dryden makes the first, and still one of the best, critical appraisal of Chaucer the poet. Here are some of the points he makes:

1, Chaucer followed Nature everywhere, but was never so bold to go beyond her.

2, As for the religion of our poet, he seems to have some little bias towards the opinions of Wycliffe, after John of Gaunt his patron; . . . yet I cannot blame him for inveighing so sharply against the vices of the clergy in his age: their pride, their ambition, their pomp, their avarice, their worldly interest, deserved the lashes which he gave them.

3, He must have been a man of a most wonderful comprehensive nature, because, as it has been truly observed of him, he has taken into the compass of his *Canterbury Tales* the various manners and humours (as we now call them) of the whole English nation, in his age.

4, 'Tis sufficient to say, according to the proverb, that here is God's plenty. We have our forefathers and great-grand-dames all before us as they were in Chaucer's days; their general characters are still remaining in mankind . . .for mankind is ever the same, and nothing is lost out of Nature, though everything is altered.

5, Chaucer, I confess, is a rough diamond, and must be first polished ere he shines.

William Blake in 1809 praises Chaucer for being 'the great poetical observer of men' and S. T. Coleridge enthuses, 'His manly cheerfulness is especially delicious to me in my old age. How exquisitely tender he is, and how perfectly free from the least touch of sickly melancholy or morbid drooping!' However, the next major critic, following Dryden, is Matthew Arnold who in his *Essays in Criticism*, published in 1888, offers these comments.

1, Chaucer's power of fascination. . .is enduring; his poetical importance does not need the assistance of the historic estimate; it is real. He is a genuine source of joy and strength, which is flowing still for us and will flow always.

2, It is by a large, free, sound representation of things, that poetry, this high criticism of life, has truth of substance; and Chaucer's poetry has truth of substance.

3, Chaucer is the father of our splendid English poetry; he is our 'well of English undefiled' because by the lovely charm of his diction, the lovely charm of his movement, he makes an epoch and founds a tradition.

4, He has poetic truth of substance, though he has not high poetic seriousness and corresponding to his truth of substance he has an exquisite virtue of style and manner. With him is born our real poetry.

Until the twentieth century, criticism was mainly in the hands of the practising poet. We now have the professional critics, often university based, who have explored Chaucer's poetry from a variety of specialised viewpoints. Many, notably Professor D. W. Robertson in *A Preface to Chaucer*, have put Chaucer into an historical context and see him as a somewhat stern medieval moral poet; others, like Professor G. L. Kittredge in *Chaucer and his Poetry*, see *The General Prologue* as a 'Human Comedy' and cite Chaucer's 'humorously sympathetic temperament'. Depending on your critic, Chaucer is either a reactionary or an innovator, a satirist, a religious writer or totally amoral. There is no shortage of lively debate.

One area of modern criticism has been extremely helpful in seeing more clearly the complexity of Chaucer's verse, its sound patterns, structural devices and tonal effects. Of outstanding importance in this respect has been the work of Nevill Coghill, who virtually re-tuned our ears to the sounds of Chaucer's language. There is also a very good little essay by E. Talbot Donaldson on *Chaucer the Pilgrim* which discusses the effects gained by using the device of a fictionalised persona to narrate the poem.

Once an artist becomes public property, his works take on the quality of an open metaphor. All kinds of interpretations jostle with each other, vying for acceptance. Most will have some kind of truth in them, provided they fit the facts of the poem, and will help us to be more aware of the qualities of intellect, feeling and craft shown by Chaucer the poet. A reading of such criticism will also show how each age stresses different areas of Chaucer's genius, but has continued to find enrichment and stimulus from a poet who is both medieval and modern.

REVISION QUESTIONS

These questions are designed to act as a stimulus to a consideration of particular aspects of Chaucer's purpose and craft, as well as offering an idea of the kind of questions to be expected in examinations.

1. 'Individuals, types, moral emblems – and some are all three.' Discuss this comment on Chaucer's characters.

2. 'The purpose of satire is the moral reform of society.' How far does this correctly describe Chaucer's purpose in *The General Prologue*?

3. 'The fact of people not practising what they preach is an unfailing source of amusement to him.' Discuss this comment as it applies to *The General Prologue*.

4. How does Chaucer avoid the danger of monotony in describing so many pilgrims one after another?

5. Determine and illustrate the varieties of humour in *The General Prologue*.

6. 'The condicioun of ech of hem. . .and whiche they weren, and of what degree, and eek in what array that they were inne.' Show how Chaucer fulfils this purpose with reference to three or four characters in *The General Prologue*.

7. 'God saw that the world was good. And God was partly right.' How far does this remark describe Chaucer's attitude to the society of his time as represented by the pilgrims?

FURTHER READING

Long book lists can be both daunting and useless, if a student cannot decide what will be of immediate interest to him. For this reason this bibliography has been kept very short. Its purpose is merely to point in one or two useful directions; further signposts are plentiful as soon as any of these books are examined.

TEXT

The standard text is still *The Works of Geoffrey Chaucer*, edited by F. N. Robinson (2nd edition, London: Oxford University Press, 1957). This contains all his known works, with useful introductions and notes, and is now available in paperback at a reasonable cost. It is a recommended purchase for all serious students of Chaucer, and a recommended reference text for all others.

INTRODUCTORY WORKS

The New Pelican Guide to English Literature, vol 1: Medieval Literature edited by Boris Ford (Penguin, 1983).

Confusingly, this volume is now published as two separate books, *Part 1* being entitled *Chaucer and the Alliterative Tradition*, *Part 2* being *The European Inheritance*. Together they give a splendid broad introduction to medieval literature with excellent anthologies of texts, and very good bibliographies.

Companion to Chaucer Studies, edited by Beryl Rowland (London: Oxford University Press, 1968).

This contains a series of chapters on all aspects of Chaucer and his background, and will guide the reader to further material on each area. The section on *The General Prologue* itself is especially good.

Geoffrey Chaucer, edited by Derek Brewer, in the series *Writers and their Background* (London: Bell, 1974).

The main value of this book is the section *A Reader's Guide to Writings on Chaucer*, which offers a helpful introduction to the often tangled world of Chaucerian studies, and gives a good sense of the different approaches to Chaucer which have been important over the years. The book also contains a long and thorough bibliography.

Chaucer and his World, by Derek Brewer (London: Eyre Methuen, 1978).

This is a very fine visual and biographical account of Chaucer and his period.

THE MACMILLAN SHAKESPEARE

General Editor: PETER HOLLINDALE
Advisory Editor: PHILIP BROCKBANK

The Macmillan Shakespeare features:
* clear and uncluttered texts with modernised punctuation and spelling wherever possible;
* full explanatory notes printed on the page facing the relevant text for ease of reference;
* stimulating introductions which concentrate on content, dramatic effect, character and imagery, rather than mere dates and sources.

Above all, The Macmillan Shakespeare treats each play as a work for the theatre which can also be enjoyed on the page.

MACMILLAN STUDENTS' NOVELS

General Editor: JAMES GIBSON

The Macmillan Students' Novels are low-priced, new editions of major classics, aimed at the first examination candidate. Each volume contains:

* enough explanation and background material to make the novels accessible — and rewarding — to pupils with little or no previous knowledge of the author or the literary period;

* detailed notes elucidate matters of vocabulary, interpretation and historical background;

* eight pages of plates comprising facsimiles of manuscripts and early editions, portraits of the author and photographs of the geographical setting of the novels.

JANE AUSTEN: MANSFIELD PARK
Editor: Richard Wirdnam

JANE AUSTEN: NORTHANGER ABBEY
Editor: Raymond Wilson

JANE AUSTEN: PRIDE AND PREJUDICE
Editor: Raymond Wilson

JANE AUSTEN: SENSE AND SENSIBILITY
Editor: Raymond Wilson

CHARLOTTE BRONTË: JANE EYRE
Editor: F. B. Pinion

EMILY BRONTË: WUTHERING HEIGHTS
Editor: Graham Handley

JOSEPH CONRAD: LORD JIM
Editor: Peter Hollindale

CHARLES DICKENS: GREAT EXPECTATIONS
Editor: James Gibson

CHARLES DICKENS: HARD TIMES
Editor: James Gibson

CHARLES DICKENS: OLIVER TWIST
Editor: Guy Williams

CHARLES DICKENS: A TALE OF TWO CITIES
Editor: James Gibson

GEORGE ELIOT: SILAS MARNER
Editor: Norman Howlings

D. H. LAWRENCE: SONS AND LOVERS
Editor: James Gibson

D. H. LAWRENCE: THE RAINBOW
Editor: James Gibson

MARK TWAIN: HUCKLEBERRY FINN
Editor: Christopher Parry

GEORGE ELIOT: MILL ON THE FLOSS
Editor: Graham Handley

JANE AUSTEN: PERSUASIAN
Editor: Richard Wirdnam

Also from Macmillan

CASEBOOK SERIES

The Macmillan *Casebook* series brings together the best of modern criticism with a selection of early reviews and comments. Each Casebook charts the development of opinion on a play, poem, or novel, or on a literary genre, from its first appearance to the present day.

GENERAL THEMES

COMEDY: DEVELOPMENTS IN CRITICISM
D. J. Palmer

DRAMA CRITICISM: DEVELOPMENTS SINCE IBSEN
A. J. Hinchliffe

THE ENGLISH NOVEL: DEVELOPMENTS IN CRITICISM SINCE HENRY JAMES
Stephen Hazell

THE LANGUAGE OF LITERATURE
N. Page

THE PASTORAL MODE
Bryan Loughrey

THE ROMANTIC IMAGINATION
J. S. Hill

TRAGEDY: DEVELOPMENTS IN CRITICISM
R. P. Draper

POETRY

WILLIAM BLAKE: SONGS OF INNOCENCE AND EXPERIENCE
Margaret Bottrall

BROWNING: MEN AND WOMEN AND OTHER POEMS
J. R. Watson

BYRON: CHILDE HAROLD'S PILGRIMAGE AND DON JUAN
John Jump

CHAUCER: THE CANTERBURY TALES
J. J. Anderson

COLERIDGE: THE ANCIENT MARINER AND OTHER POEMS
A. R. Jones and W. Tydeman

DONNE: SONGS AND SONETS
Julian Lovelock

T. S. ELIOT: FOUR QUARTERS
Bernard Bergonzi

T. S. ELIOT: PRUFROCK, GERONTION, ASH WEDNESDAY AND OTHER POEMS
B. C. Southam

T. S. ELIOT: THE WASTELAND
C. B. Cox and A. J. Hinchliffe

ELIZABETHAN POETRY: LYRICAL AND NARRATIVE

Gerald Hammond
THOMAS HARDY: POEMS
J. Gibson and T. Johnson

GERALD MANLEY HOPKINS: POEMS
Margaret Bottrall

KEATS: ODES
G. S. Fraser

KEATS: THE NARRATIVE POEMS
J. S. Hill

MARVELL: POEMS
Arthur Pollard

THE METAPHYSICAL POETS
Gerald Hammond

MILTON: COMUS AND SAMSON
AGONISTES
Julian Lovelock

MILTON: PARADISE LOST
A. E. Dyson and Julian Lovelock

POETRY OF THE FIRST WORLD
WAR
Dominic Hibberd

ALEXANDER POPE: THE RAPE OF
THE LOCK
John Dixon Hunt

SHELLEY: SHORTER POEMS &
LYRICS
Patrick Swinden

SPENSER: THE FAERIE QUEEN
Peter Bayley

TENNYSON: IN MEMORIAM
John Dixon Hunt

THIRTIES POETS: 'THE AUDEN
GROUP'
Ronald Carter

WORDSWORTH: LYRICAL
BALLADS
A. R. Jones and W. Tydeman

WORDSWORTH: THE PRELUDE
W. J. Harvey and R. Gravil

W. B. YEATS: POEMS 1919–1935
E. Cullingford

W. B. YEATS: LAST POEMS
Jon Stallworthy

THE NOVEL AND PROSE

JANE AUSTEN: EMMA
David Lodge

JANE AUSTEN: NORTHANGER
ABBEY AND PERSUASION
B. C. Southam

JANE AUSTEN: SENSE AND
SENSIBILITY, PRIDE AND
PREJUDICE AND MANSFIELD
PARK
B. C. Southam

CHARLOTTE BRONTË: JANE EYRE
AND VILLETTE
Miriam Allott

EMILY BRONTË: WUTHERING
HEIGHTS
Miriam Allott

BUNYAN: THE PILGRIM'S
PROGRESS
R. Sharrock

CONRAD: HEART OF DARKNESS,
NOSTROMO AND UNDER
WESTERN EYES
C. B. Cox

CONRAD: THE SECRET AGENT
Ian Watt

CHARLES DICKENS: BLEAK
HOUSE
A. E. Dyson

CHARLES DICKENS: HARD TIMES,
GREAT EXPECTATIONS AND OUR
MUTUAL FRIEND
N. Page

GEORGE ELIOT: MIDDLEMARCH
Patrick Swinden

GEORGE ELIOT: THE MILL ON
THE FLOSS AND SILAS MARNER
R. P. Draper

HENRY FIELDING: TOM JONES
Neil Compton

E. M. FORSTER: A PASSAGE TO
INDIA
Malcolm Bradbury

HARDY: THE TRAGIC NOVELS
R. P. Draper

HENRY JAMES: WASHINGTON
SQUARE AND THE PORTRAIT OF
A LADY
Alan Shelston

JAMES JOYCE: DUBLINERS AND A
PORTRAIT OF THE ARTIST AS A
YOUNG MAN
Morris Beja

D. H. LAWRENCE: THE RAINBOW
AND WOMEN IN LOVE
Colin Clarke

D. H. LAWRENCE: SONS AND
LOVERS
Gamini Salgado

SWIFT: GULLIVER'S TRAVELS
Richard Gravil

THACKERAY: VANITY FAIR
Arthur Pollard

TROLLOPE: THE BARSETSHIRE
NOVELS
T. Bareham

VIRGINIA WOOLF: TO THE
LIGHTHOUSE
Morris Beja

DRAMA

CONGREVE: COMEDIES
Patrick Lyons

T. S. ELIOT: PLAYS
Arnold P. Hinchliffe

JONSON: EVERY MAN IN HIS
HUMOUR AND THE ALCHEMIST
R. V. Holdsworth

JONSON: VOLPONE
J. A. Barish

MARLOWE: DR. FAUSTUS
John Jump

MARLOWE: TAMBURLAINE,
EDWARD II AND THE JEW OF
MALTA
John Russell Brown

MEDIEVAL ENGLISH DRAMA
Peter Happé

O'CASEY: JUNO AND THE
PAYCOCK, THE PLOUGH AND THE
STARS AND THE SHADOW OF A
GUNMAN
R. Ayling

JOHN OSBORNE: LOOK BACK IN
ANGER
John Russell Taylor

WEBSTER: THE WHITE DEVIL AND
THE DUCHESS OF MALFI
R. V. Holdsworth

WILDE: COMEDIES
W. Tydeman

SHAKESPEARE

SHAKESPEARE: ANTONY AND
CLEOPATRA
John Russell Brown

SHAKESPEARE: CORIOLANUS
B. A. Brockman

SHAKESPEARE: HAMLET
John Jump

SHAKESPEARE: HENRY IV PARTS
I AND II
G. K. Hunter

SHAKESPEARE: HENRY V
Michael Quinn

SHAKESPEARE: JULIUS CAESAR
Peter Ure

SHAKESPEARE: KING LEAR
Frank Kermode

SHAKESPEARE: MACBETH
John Wain

SHAKESPEARE: MEASURE FOR
MEASURE
G. K. Stead

SHAKESPEARE: THE MERCHANT
OF VENICE
John Wilders

SHAKESPEARE: A MIDSUMMER
NIGHT'S DREAM
A. W. Price

SHAKESPEARE: MUCH ADO
ABOUT NOTHING AND AS YOU
LIKE IT
John Russell Brown

SHAKESPEARE: OTHELLO
John Wain

SHAKESPEARE: RICHARD II
N. Brooke

SHAKESPEARE: THE SONNETS
Peter Jones

SHAKESPEARE: THE TEMPEST
D. J. Palmer

SHAKESPEARE: TROILUS AND
CRESSIDA
Priscilla Martin

SHAKESPEARE: TWELFTH NIGHT
D. J. Palmer

SHAKESPEARE: THE WINTER'S
TALE
Kenneth Muir

MACMILLAN SHAKESPEARE VIDEO WORKSHOPS

DAVID WHITWORTH

Two unique book and video packages, one on tragedy and the other on comedy, each offering insights into four plays. Designed for all students of Shakespeare, each package assumes no previous knowledge of the plays and can serve as a useful introduction to Shakespeare for 'O' and 'A' level candidates as well as for students at colleges and institutes of further, higher and adult education.

The material is based on the New Shakespeare Company Workshops at the Roundhouse, adapted and extended for television. By combining the resources of television and a small theatre company, this exploration of Shakespeare's plays offers insights into varied interpretations, presentation, styles of acting as well as useful background information.

While being no substitute for seeing the whole plays in performance, it is envisaged that these video cassettes will impart something of the original excitement of the theatrical experience, and serve as a welcome complement to textual analysis leading to an enriched and broader view of the plays.

Each package consists of:

* the Macmillan Shakespeare editions of the plays concerned;

* a video cassette available in VHS or Beta;

* a leaflet of teacher's notes.

THE TORTURED MIND
looks at the four tragedies Hamlet, Othello, Macbeth and King Lear.

THE COMIC SPIRIT
examines the comedies Much Ado About Nothing, Twelfth Night, A Midsummer Night's Dream, and As You Like It.